Praise for
The Biting Solution: The Expert's Guide for Parents, Caregivers, and Early Childhood Educators

A great "guide-by-your-side" resource that offers a wealth of information in an easy to read and accessible way. It's surprising that a book with such a specific focus can have such broad applications; this book could be used for a variety of challenging behaviors, with a variety of populations. Ms. Poelle's approach and strategies demonstrate not only a solid knowledge of early childhood development, but also a terrific grasp of how adults learn, giving them the tools they need to help children make changes that are effective and genuine.

> —SUSAN EINBENDER, *parent adviser, Early Intervention at Pennsylvania School for the Deaf*

As managing director of more than 20 preschools and an educator for 17 years, I have never seen such an effective tool for dealing with socially unacceptable behaviors as The Biting Solution. *I have personally witnessed complete behavioral transformations in students who were once deemed problematic. An invaluable resource for all parents and teachers.*

> —JILL HOWARD, *executive director, Preschool of America*

A must-have book for parents and teachers of young children. . . . The examples of actual situations and customized solutions clearly illustrate how to use this method with children of different ages. A great tool for anyone living or working with young children!

> —STEPHANIE DOCKWEILER, M.A., *president, QS2 Training and Consulting*

As the child care center director of many programs, I have consistently used Lisa Poelle's advice in tackling a myriad of challenges. I highly recommend her book to both early childhood educators and parents.

> —JOAN CAMPANELLA-SHUTT, *child care center director*

Sound advice about how to eliminate hurtful behavior . . . which is often misunderstood and not always respectfully extinguished. A must-read for childcare providers, parents of young children, and parents of twins.

> —DIANNE THOMAS, *licensed marriage and family therapist, twins specialist, and parent educator*

Wow! Great book! Parents and teachers get a better understanding of why young children resort to hurting each other, plus effective, concrete ideas to prevent and respond to these problem behaviors.

> —LAUREN KUEHN, *director, Green Hills Pre-School*

Lisa Poelle's firm, warm writing style calms and empowers parents and educational professionals.

> —JENNIFER BUTCH, *early childhood educator, NYC Early Childhood Professional Development Institute*

[The Biting Solution] *provides very effective and wise solutions that work.*

> —ELLEN GALINSKY, *president, Families and Work Institute; author,* Mind in the Making: The Seven Essential Skills Every Child Needs

The Biting Solution

The Expert's No-Biting Guide for Parents, Caregivers, and Early Childhood Educators

Lisa Poelle, M.A.

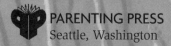

PARENTING PRESS
Seattle, Washington

Printed in the United States of America

Edited by Carolyn J. Threadgill
Designed by Judy Petry

ISBN 978-1-936903-07-8

Library of Congress Cataloging-in-Publication Data

Poelle, Lisa 1955-
    The Biting Solution : The Expert's No-Biting Guide for Parents, Caregivers, and Early Childhood Educators / Lisa Poelle, M.A. – 1ˢᵗ edition.
        pages cm
    Includes bibliographical references and index.
    ISBN 978-1-936903-07-8 (pbk.)
    1. Child rearing. 2. Parenting. I. Title.
    HQ769.P7864 2012
    649'.1–dc23

                                                                    2012027456

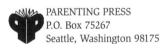 PARENTING PRESS
P.O. Box 75267
Seattle, Washington 98175

To see all of our helpful publications and services for parents, caregivers, and children, go to www.ParentingPress.com.

Dedication

I dedicate this book to my husband
with whom I fell deeply in love when I was but a teenager.
Thank you, Mark, for your endless support, adventuresome spirit,
and unconditional love.

Contents

Foreword

Early childhood is a time of tremendous growth. It is an exciting period when new skills seem to appear every day. It is also a time, however, when young children's behavior can be difficult for adults to understand—especially when it is persistent and hurtful. The goal of fostering respect for others may seem far away when biting and fighting demand center stage. Parents, teachers, and child care providers need help to understand some of the *challenging* behaviors of early childhood. Lisa Poelle's book, *The Biting Solution,* provides that support and understanding and helps take the mystery out of misbehavior.

Toddlers and young preschoolers, the age group focused on in this book, are learning significant motor, language, and social skills like sharing, helping, and cooperating. They are also learning important emotional skills like empathy and self-reliance. It's little wonder that, for some of them, frustrations can surface quickly and anger may seem out of control. Giving parents and child care providers guides from a developmental perspective can help them understand what may be causing *difficult* behavior. Encouraging them to quickly apply and use what they have learned is a unique feature embedded within the book.

The Biting Solution is written in a conversational and supportive style. A *process* is introduced that encourages adults to communicate regularly, collect child observations, and develop an Action Plan. Adults work together for the benefit of the child. Simplistic explanations like "she's teething" or "he'll grow out of it" are avoided. The book reminds readers that there is never one clear reason for a particular behavior, and seeking an answer by jumping to the wrong conclusion only creates more frustration.

This book reflects Lisa Poelle's years of experience as a guidance consultant to parents and early childhood educators. It reflects her strong commitment to a practical, problem-solving approach to help adults deal with young children's behaviors that are volatile, repetitive, and aggressive. The book is written in a fact-finding versus fault-finding manner, consistently considering solutions that are objective and age appropriate. Biting, especially, can be a behavior that is laden with guilt and shame . . . for *all* involved. *The Biting Solution* provides adults with tools to deal with difficult behavior in a collaborative and pro-active way.

—Dianne W. Eyer, professor emerita
Early Childhood Education and Child Development
Cañada College, Redwood City, California
Co-author, Infants, Toddlers and Caregivers, *9th edition*

Acknowledgments

Many thanks to the people who had a special impact on my professional growth, as well as those who supported me while I wrote this book:

All of the parents, teachers, and caregivers who over the years have shared their stories and struggles with me.

Elizabeth Jones, my Master's degree advisor at Pacific Oaks College: Her insightful stories, thoughtful teaching, and emphasis on authentic personal reflection helped me learn many valuable lessons about myself and my field.

Children's Health Council, Palo Alto, California: I spent ten years at this multidisciplinary agency working as a parent educator, child care consultant, and mentoring program director. The lessons I learned through my experiences working with the caring professionals at this agency shaped my professional growth and formed the bedrock of my understanding of human development. It was a learning environment like no other, and I am eternally grateful for the opportunity.

Dianne Thomas, my colleague and office mate for ten years: I will never forget our many poignant conversations about difficult cases and fascinating people. Thank you for proofreading my manuscript and sharing your insights and perspectives.

Debbie Cohen, my colleague and long-time friend: Your expertise on staff development, program design, and leadership issues has been invaluable to me.

Carolyn Kelso, my mom: Thank you for thoughtfully proofreading my manuscript early in the process and for always supporting me emotionally with your loving embrace, even from afar.

Craig Kelso, my dad, and my sons, **Travis** and **Tyler:** I have always felt your pride in me throughout the long journey of writing this book.

Barbara Poelle, my daughter-in-law: I appreciate the special expertise you shared with me to help me learn to navigate the world of publishing.

Carolyn Threadgill, my editor: Thank you from the bottom of my heart for your faith and expertise in bringing this project to fruition.

How to Use This Book

As a guidance consultant to parents and early childhood educators, much of my work has focused on helping to solve the mystery of a young child's frequent biting episodes as quickly as possible. In most cases, an ultimatum has been given to parents by the program: get the biting to stop or the child will be expelled from the group. Typically, parents are given two to three weeks to accomplish this daunting task.

The Biting Solution will prepare you to deal expertly with having a biting child in your midst, whether it is in your own family, a play group, a child care center, a part-day preschool, or any other kind of early childhood program. No longer will you be caught off guard by the firestorm of emotions that accompany biting. Based on what I've learned through my experiences with many children who bite, I've developed a process for dealing successfully with this volatile issue. *In fact, it works for all types of hurtful behaviors.*

The children

All the techniques in *The Biting Solution* are equally useful for working or living with typically developing children and those with identified *special needs*. Adults who work with children who have special needs must strive to become especially clear and consistent in their responses to various challenging behaviors.

The communication techniques described in this book will help parents and caregivers hone their skills so that children can learn what is expected of them more readily. *Instructive Intervention* (page 19) is an effective tool for helping adults gain consistency and clarity in their responses to all children.

The *Seven Questions* (page 12) offer a useful perspective on interpreting a wide variety of factors influencing a child's behavior. Where special needs are involved (for example, autism spectrum disorders or Down Syndrome), the questions regarding social/emotional development, verbal skills, physical condition, and the nature of the physical environment will be particularly helpful in figuring out the cause of the biting problem. In addition, every "How to Help the Child" section provides specific, proven ways for adults to help prevent meltdowns.

Children with special needs require an extraordinary amount of patience from the adults in their lives, and those adults require an extraordinary amount of resources and support. *The Biting Solution* offers such assistance to all adults who work or live with young children, those who are typically developing, those with identified special needs, or those for whom you sense something "more" is needed even when you don't know the reason.

The process

The process I use involves child observations, communication among parents, teachers, and caregivers, and design of a customized *Action Plan* with a role for everyone to play.

When interviewing adults about when and how the hurtful behavior occurs, I find that everyone always has a theory about why it is happening. Very few have a concrete plan for making changes. Typically, adults believe the problem lies within the child. Adults are perennially frustrated when the child won't "mind them" or "play nice" with others. They explain the behavior by saying: "She just doesn't want to listen," or "he's teething," or "her parents keep her up too late at night," or he "lacks verbal skills," etc. Adults usually pin the child's behavior on one "reason" and leave it at that. Rarely do they ever consider the potential benefits of changing their own behavior, the daily schedule, or the child's environment. Often, miscommunication or complete lack of communication between parents and caregivers clouds the issues and creates unnecessary obstacles to behavioral changes.

Think like a consultant

All adults—parents, teachers, and caregivers—will be most effective when they set aside their own personal point of view and, instead, learn how to "think like a consultant." Whenever a child is struggling with biting or other hurtful behavior, adults can learn how to do observations and interviews that will uncover reasons for the behavior. In doing so, they'll take the mystery out of the misbehavior. Whether parent or early childhood professional, adults can learn to recognize and reduce stressors, set reasonable limits, and promote pro-social behavior. As you will discover, most changes need to be made by the adults. Each chapter offers specific ways for them to adjust their own behavior and alter the setting, to create a better fit for the child at home and for the children in group care. I have found that these lessons can be learned and applied fairly quickly, regardless of past experience. Consider me the newest member of your support team as you learn to solve biting problems.

What to do the minute biting happens

Part I deals with hurtful behavior from various adults' points of view. The first chapter focuses on how people feel and behave when there is a child who bites. The second chapter demonstrates Instructive Intervention, a technique to be used *as soon as hurtful behavior occurs* at home or in an early childhood program.

Solving biting issues with the Seven Questions

Part II asks the Seven Questions, the core of the book, whose answers will shed light on reasons behind a child's behavior. Thinking about your own child or a specific child in group care while reading these chapters will help you think concretely. Each chapter will include specific solutions targeted to your needs.

Intervention in action

Part III presents five case studies to illustrate how this process was actually used with young children at various ages. In the first section of each case study I provide background information about the family, early childhood program, and the history of the misbehavior. Next, you will find notes from my observations and interviews based on the Seven Questions. Last, you will read the customized Action Plan that I and the other adults developed and used for each case. I think it will be extremely useful for you to see this tool in action. The three age groups shown in case studies are toddlers (15-24 months), two-year-olds, and three-year-olds.

The Seven Questions

1. How much of the child's behavior is related to typical social/emotional development?
2. What past experiences or recent changes may be creating stress?
3. Is the lack of verbal skills causing frustration?
4. Is the child's physical condition a contributing factor?
5. What role does the child's temperament play in the behavior?
6. What effect does the physical environment of the home or early childhood program have on the child?
7. What kind of limit setting is the child experiencing at home and with other caregivers or teachers?

Creating your "Action Plan"

Part IV provides an opportunity for you to design your own customized Action Plan, a blueprint for the actions adults need to take to reduce a child's stressors and set the stage for success. After three or four days of implementing your plan, you should have started to see a reduction in biting *if the changes are in place and consistently applied.* In a week, you should see dramatic reduction. By two weeks, the child's biting will very likely be a thing of the past. If your child is still frequently hurting others after three weeks, the child may have a more serious underlying problem that needs a thorough evaluation by a developmental or medical expert. In that case, the insights you have gathered through this process will be extremely useful to those professionals.

Ready? Let's get started!

Part I

Adults' Feelings and Actions

Biting:
A Tremendous Challenge

Biting is one of the most challenging behavior problems faced by parents and caregivers. Even the most experienced of early childhood educators struggle with persistent biting among toddlers, twos, and young preschoolers. A child who frequently bites creates severe stress for adults and can wreak havoc on an entire family or early childhood program. No other type of childhood aggression engenders the same kind of reaction from adults. Other children may be aggressive by pushing, kicking, hitting, or scratching, but they rarely get kicked out of the program for these behaviors. Biting, on the other hand, raises a huge red flag. Parents of both the child who bites and the child who is bitten are frantic and desperate for a speedy solution.

Any Child Can Become a Biter

▶ Ethan, an active and happy eighteen-month-old with a broad smile and an outgoing personality, had been biting others at child care for three months.

▶ Sophia, a highly verbal twenty-one-month-old with a challenging temperament, attempted to bite other children at child care on a daily basis.

▶ Lukas, a mild-mannered, nonverbal two-year-old, attended his mother's company child care center, biting her co-worker's children nearly every day.

▶ Elijah, a verbal and intellectually precocious three-year-old who attended a bilingual child care center, attempted to bite his classmates several times a day.

▶ Mia, a three-and-a half-year-old with autism, bit newcomers to the program.

Parents and caregivers must work together

Dealing with a child who bites engenders a slew of difficult feelings, from blame and shame to confusion and anger. All of these can inhibit effective responses. Ideally, all adults who work with a child who bites will empathize with each other. They will act in a concerted, cohesive manner, leaving behind their own emotional baggage. It is important to appreciate and acknowledge each other's point of view and work together for the child's benefit. *Using this book together* will provide a road map for combining your efforts, making real progress to help the child and resolve the situation.

Track record for solving biting challenges

I am happy to say that throughout my consulting practice, when teachers and parents have used the methods in this book honestly and consistently, biting cases were resolved positively and very quickly.

While most of this book focuses on biting, these same techniques can be applied to any type of hurtful behavior. In fact, even if they aren't concerned with biting, parents, caregivers, and teachers will find valuable information for understanding young children, as well as many techniques for proactively preventing various problem behaviors from ever developing. As I always say, if you can handle biting, you can handle anything!

Life with toddlers and twos

Toddlers and twos are relentlessly curious about other people, but at this age, they have little concept of anyone else's needs and wants. They are truly self-centered. When things don't go for them as expected, depending on their personality some are prone to act out or fight back through physical actions that can prove seriously hurtful to others. Impulse control is immature at this stage of development. Given certain circumstances, some children begin to rely on biting or aggression as a typical reaction to stress, especially in group settings.

Being with toddlers and two-year-olds is much like being on a rollercoaster ride, whether you are the parent, caregiver, or teacher. It can be awfully tough to maintain your balance. It's hard to be completely prepared for what you will find around the next bend. While children at this age are often hysterically funny and exhilarating to be around, you literally cannot take your eyes off of them because they are so likely to inadvertently get into trouble. Even though they have no concept of safety and don't know their physical limitations, they now have the physical capability to get pretty much anywhere on their own steam in a split second. It is exhausting trying to keep up with their boundless energy and curious nature! While they become more energetic, we grow more tired. Maybe toddlers have so much energy because they magically drain it right out of the adults in their lives!

How parents of children who bite feel

Parents are typically embarrassed by their child's behavior and at a loss as to how to stop it. Being responsible for behavior they cannot control is incredibly distressing. They may even feel ostracized by other parents. Some parents of children who bite overreact by instituting rigid punishments at home, continuing them long after the incident has passed. Others take the offensive,

Getting Parents on Board

When you are caring for a child who is hurtful to others, you want to get the parent(s) working together with you to solve the problem. Set up a time to talk privately. Bring notes from your observations and some initial ideas for stopping the behavior. Set the parent's mind at ease by being friendly and collaborative.

You might say, "Thanks for coming in today to meet with me about Conner. As you know, we love having Conner here. Right now we're worried about how he often bites children. Of course, some biting is a common occurrence in programs with young children. When it happens frequently with an individual child, however, it's a signal that it's time for us to take a closer look.

So, that's the purpose of our meeting today. I feel confident that through working together, we can figure out how to help Conner stop biting. Since you know Conner better than anyone, your point of view and involvement is critical to our success. I have found that using the Seven Questions [give parent a copy of the questions] gives us a clear problem-solving format. It's a good way to get to the heart of the issues so we can design a plan of action that will be exactly what Conner needs. Make sense?"

casting all blame on caregivers or on the early childhood program. Some may jump to the conclusion that their child has developmental issues. And others are ashamed, apologetic, and grateful to be in a program at all under these circumstances, bending over backwards to take any advice offered.

Some parents had their child evicted from child care before or have gone through several nannies. They may be afraid of losing their job, having had to miss many days of work due to lengthy child care searches. They may be worried about their child's social development, since these children are often shunned by other families, not invited to birthday parties and weekend playdates. While at work, parents may live in constant fear of getting another call from the caregiver asking to them to pick up the child who bit . . . again. Or, at the end of the day, they may feel anxious to encounter yet another incident report and the accompanying glare of the other parents.

How parents of bitten children feel

These parents may be outraged by their child's injury and concerned about permanent scarring, infection, or disease. They feel terrible because they are unable to protect their child and anxious about what they will encounter at the end of each day. At work, they live in fear of getting another call from the nanny or early childhood program, reporting yet another incident. Feelings of blame are common, as are concerns that they are not being taken seriously. Caregivers may have tried to calm them down by saying how normal and common biting is in groups of young children. Parents often hear this as a "wait-it-out" policy, with their child unwittingly acting as the bait for other children who are learning not to bite.

Some parents see biting as a deliberate act of aggression against their child; they want decisive action. They feel desperate and may want a guarantee from the child care program that their child will be protected from the child who bites, even separated from that child during play. They may demand that the biting child be punished in a certain fashion, suspended, or even expelled.

When biting happens at home while parents are taking care of two siblings or two friends, parents

---

Getting Teachers on Board

As the parent of a child who is hurtful to others, you want to get the caregivers/teachers to work with you. Ask to have a private meeting with both the director of the program and your child's main caregiver or teacher. Come prepared with notes about your point of view concerning your child's biting. Be friendly and collaborative: everyone will have the same goal to work as a team on behalf of your child and the other children.

You might say, "Thanks for meeting with me about Daniella today. As you know, I love having Daniella attend your program. Right now, I'm worried about how often she bites others. While I know that small children commonly bite when stressed, I want to work with you to find a way to reduce her stressors and increase her ability to handle herself without biting.

I've recently discovered a book that focuses on biting, and I'd like to suggest that we work as a team and use this book to help Daniella and the other children. In this book there are Seven Questions [give everyone a copy of the Seven Questions] to ask ourselves to get at the root of the problem. I'm more than willing to do whatever I can to help. I hope we can get started on this together right away. Sound good?"

may feel incredibly guilty and frustrated. There they are on site at the time of the bite, but may be unable to stop it from happening.

How those who take care of children feel

Caregivers, teachers, and directors of early childhood programs may be stumped by chronic biting problems. They may be about to give an ultimatum to the family, expelling the child if she or he can't stop biting soon. These professionals are in a particularly tough position. They are trying to meet the needs of all of the clients: the children, the parents of the child who bites, and the parents of the victim. They care deeply about the children in their program. And, of course, they also want to alleviate the situation as soon as possible before they lose customers and their reputation suffers.

Nannies, family child care providers, or babysitters are only a "force of one" when dealing with behavior problems. They feel especially vulnerable and alone when trying to deal with a persistent biting problem.

Whatever your role, *you are not alone.* Few adults feel comfortable handling this extremely challenging behavior, but together we can change that.

"We Don't Put Our Teeth on People!"

One night I got a phone call from a client of mine, Susan. She apologized for calling me in the evening, but explained that she needed to share an experience she just had with her 21-month-old daughter Lily. That evening Susan had been sharing a bubble bath with Lily. At one point, Susan had reached under the bubbles to find Lily's toes, leaning over to playfully nibble on them, saying "Yummy, I love toes!" All of a sudden, Lily stood upright in the tub, hands on hips, shouting at her mother, "Mommy, we don't put our teeth on people!"

Susan told me she was embarrassed to have been set straight by her toddler. She was also thrilled that her daughter had internalized a lesson we had been trying to teach her, to avoid her getting booted out of child care for her constant biting. On my website *www.stopthefightingandbiting.com* there are links to two original children's songs written by Travis and Barbara Poelle of The 2 Tones, which will help your child internalize these new lessons: "We Don't Put Our Teeth on People" and "Someone You Love (The Hug Song)." Lyrics to these songs can be found on pages 122–123 of this book.

Responding to Biting When It Happens

Most people who live or work with young children are always on the lookout for ideas on how to intervene effectively *during conflicts* between children. This chapter recommends effective ways to deal with these incidents, either at the point of the attempt or right after the incident has occurred. I call this *Instructive Intervention.*

In later chapters, I will explain how to ask the right questions to get at the roots of the biting problem. Coupling my Instructive Intervention technique immediately with proper detective work later through the Seven Questions will be the secret to your success.

Out with the old, before bringing in the new

Let's look at ineffective responses and why they don't work. You will replace these with Instructive Intervention (page 19).

Excessive reactions

Extreme misbehavior, such as biting, engenders a strong reaction from adults. They can feel baffled and helpless by children's violent outbursts. Often, adults are actually within arm's reach of the children at play and biting suddenly happens, right under their nose.

Adults sometimes find themselves ranting and lecturing when incidents happen. They feel incredibly tense and angry and try to make an impression about the *seriousness of the crime.* "How could you do that to your friend, Jose? How many times have I told you we don't hurt our friends? You know how to talk. Why can't you use your words? I can't believe this keeps happening!" These tirades give adults a chance to vent, but they can really ratchet up the stress level in the room. They cloud the issue by combining shame and guilt with a heavy dose of anger. Such an emotional performance can overwhelm the child, taking the focus away from the learning opportunities. Indeed, a strong, clear response is called for, one that is matter-of-fact, simple to follow, and calm.

Reasoning with the child

The most common response to hurtful behavior is the classic question, "How would you like it if someone did that to you?" Inevitably, toddlers look away uncomfortably and two-year-olds may say that they wouldn't like it. Continuing with what they think is a logical approach, adults say something like, "Well, then, you shouldn't do it to anyone else, either. It's not nice." Though perfectly reasonable to adults, this seemingly logical construction of thought means little to young children. Even if they appear to buy into the rationale for not hurting the other child, they haven't received any useful tools for the next time they are confronted with similar stressors. While it is admirable to teach children to care about each other's feelings, this kind of inappropriate reasoning is not a discipline technique. It is no wonder that adults remain so confounded at the persistence of biting and fighting when this is their main recourse.

Putting toddlers in time-out

Some adults punish children with a time-out as a consequence for various infractions. In this technique, children are restricted to a particular spot for a set period of time, depriving them of the adult's attention. As a general rule, the child is sequestered this way for one minute per year of age. Time-outs can be successfully used with many preschoolers, but they are of limited value with children under the age of two and a half, who often see time-out as no more than simply a feature of their biting "routine." (They are also of limited or no value for children with special needs.) In fact, when biting is a frequent occurrence, many toddlers bite and then calmly *walk themselves over to the time-out spot* to pay penance for their crime. For them, it seems the crime is worth the punishment, frustrating parents and caregivers that much more.

Though a biting child should immediately be separated from the victim and other children, the adult's overarching message should be, "It is my job to keep people *safe,* so I can't let you *near people* right now" rather than a provocative "You're in *big* trouble now, buddy. Get in time-out!" Remember, the more concrete your message, the better it will be understood by young children.

Isolating children

Isolating the child who bites from the group for prolonged periods or all day may seem like a good solution on the surface, but it addresses only the short-term need. Children who act out still need to be around other children in order to learn alternatives to their biting. Of course, this requires careful supervision by adults. This behavioral experience is necessary to reinforce behavioral changes. Only when parents and caregivers do their part to reduce stressors and model effective responses can children learn new strategies to deal with their problems and get along better with others.

What to Say and Do Instead

Instructive Intervention

Instructive Intervention is a short, to-the-point technique for dealing with biting the moment it occurs. It has seven parts:

1. Interrupt the behavior.
2. Help the child who was bitten.
3. Reflect both children's feelings.
4. Define the problem.
5. Clarify the limit.
6. Provide solutions.
7. Re-engage in play.

When used consistently, this technique is very helpful to children who lack skills to solve their own problem. It also provides security for them as there is obviously an adult around who knows what to do every time there is a problem.

Instructive Intervention tools

On page 21, you will find the "Instructive Intervention Guide," the sequence of steps to deal with biting immediately. Keep a copy of this page near you for quick reference when biting occurs. It will help you be consistent and effective.

The "Puppet Show Script" on page 22 is a parent or teacher tool you can use anytime when children are calm and likely to be receptive to new information. You will teach children some ways to handle intense feelings without biting. Role play like this really captures young children's attention—"live" entertainment on a familiar topic, as it were.

Practice makes it easier

Practice what you plan to say during future biting incidents. Photocopy and laminate the Biting Solution Pocket Guide on page 121 to distribute to staff and parents. Invite others to watch the use of newly acquired techniques and discuss the process together. Be patient while people learn a new style of intervention. Using unfamiliar phrases and messages will feel uncomfortable at first. Modeling effective intervention with a partner or colleagues is a helpful way to share information concretely.

Getting to the root of the problem

Seven Questions

Moving on to Part II, you will find a discussion and how-to of the Seven Questions that will help you get to the root of the biting problem. At the end of each of the next seven short chapters, you will check off the issues that pertain to the child who is biting. This information will provide the foundation for your customized Action Plan in due course.

Injury and Incident Reports

Also useful are Injury and Incident reports. Unfortunately, often an Injury Report form is filled out by caregivers in a rather perfunctory manner, only recording information of *when* and *how* the victim was hurt and a description of the *care* provided afterward. It is best when adults can write a clear description of the play situation *prior to the injury*, to capture vital information for solving the problem. (Frequently there are no details recorded on these forms specifically about the child who bites. The biter's identity is typically kept confidential because these forms may be given to the injured child's parents.)

If your child bites, ask to see all of the Injury and Incident reports. See if you can detect any patterns,

---

Treating a Bite Wound

If the skin is not broken, there is no cause for concern of infection. The site of the bite will be painful, and after you wash it off with soap and water, put ice or ice packs on it. You can also use frozen sponges or ice wrapped in washcloths. Small bags of frozen peas in a clean cloth or plastic bag are also popular because they conform to the shape of the body.

▶ First wash your own hands and then wash the wound with warm, soapy water.

After the wound is cleaned, it is best if you can leave it exposed to open air for a while. If you are concerned it may get dirt in it, cover it with a bandage.

▶ In a bite that *breaks the skin* on the fingers or hands, bacteria may come into contact with tendons. When such bites occur, *children should be seen by medical personnel*. The situation is not an emergency, but the child should see a doctor as soon as possible.

INSTRUCTIVE INTERVENTION GUIDE

1. Interrupt the behavior:
- *"No biting. Sit down right here in this spot. We'll talk about it in a minute."*

2. Help the victim:
- *"I know that really hurt. Here, let me help you feel better."*

3. Reflect both children's feelings:
- *[To child who bit] "I can see that you felt frustrated and angry."*
- *[To child who was bitten] "And you felt scared and then sad."*

4. Define the problem:
- *"I see the problem—you both wanted to play with the same doll at the very same time. That was the problem."*

5. Clarify the limit:
- *"We always touch people gently, even when we're upset or angry. If you hurt people, you'll have to stay next to me. I won't let you play with the children when you hurt them."*

6. Provide two relevant solutions, one for expressing feelings and one for expressing needs. Select and offer a suggestion that might appeal to the child:
- *"When you feel upset, you can show that by . . . "*
  - ▶ Telling the other person how you feel
  - ▶ Taking big, deep breaths
  - ▶ Clenching your teeth, making a grrrr sound
  - ▶ Putting your hands on your hips
  - ▶ Squeezing your fists
  - ▶ Folding your arms across your chest
- *"If you need something, you can say to the other child . . . "*
  - ▶ "I need the next turn."
  - ▶ "I'm waiting for the next turn."
  - ▶ "How many minutes until you're done?"
  - ▶ "Can I play with you?"
  - ▶ "Want to trade that for this . . . ?"
  - ▶ "Can you bring it to me when you're done? I'll be over there."

  For toddlers, suggest shorter phrases they can manage:
  - ▶ "My turn?"
  - ▶ "Mine now?"
  - ▶ "I want that."
  - ▶ "Be careful!"

7. Put closure on the situation and re-engage in play:
- *"I'm glad to see that you are all done biting. Let's go do . . . "*

PUPPET SHOW SCRIPT

This script is a tool for teachers and parents to use in illustrating how children can deal with the difficult feelings that arise in hurtful incidents. You will need two puppets or stuffed animals and one toy/item small enough for a puppet to hold. One adult can operate both puppets, while another adult plays the role of "Teacher."

Dog: *"Hey, look!"* [Shakes a tambourine]

Bear: [Runs over to Dog] *"I want that!"* [Grabs at tambourine]

Dog: *"Augghh!"* [Screams, struggling to hold on]

Bear: *"No . . . It's mine!"* [Bear bites Dog's paw and Dog lets go]

Dog: [Cries]

Teacher: *"What's going on over here? Bear, sit down and stay right here. I can't let you play near Dog when you hurt him."* [Teacher separates Bear from Dog. She goes over to Dog and pretends to wash his paw and put ice on it]

Teacher: *"Oh, Dog, I'll bet you felt scared and sad. Here is some nice cold ice to make your paw feel better. I'm sorry you were hurt. Listen, Dog, here is an idea for you. When someone tries to take something from you, you can say, 'No' or 'Stop' in a loud voice. Can you try that?* [Dog says 'Stop' loudly] *Yes, that's great! Let's go talk to Bear now."*

Teacher: *"Bear, we need to talk about what happened. You felt mad at Dog because he wouldn't give you the tambourine."*

Bear: *"I wanted it!"* [Bear shouts at Dog]

Teacher: *"Right, you did. Then, Dog felt scared when you grabbed it and sad when you hurt him."*

Dog: *"I don't like that!"* [Dog screams at Bear]

Teacher: *"Right, you didn't like that. So, Bear, the problem is you really wanted the tambourine that Dog was using. It's hard to wait for a turn. But even when we're upset or mad, we still touch others gently."*

Bear: *"Hummph!"* [Looks away, still feeling unhappy]

Teacher: *"Listen, Bear, I have an idea for you. When you want a toy that someone else has you can take big belly breaths to calm yourself while you wait. Watch me take a belly breath: I'm going to breathe in and blow out my mad feelings.* [Teacher takes a deep breath, then blows out as long as possible] *Let's all practice belly breaths.* [Teacher, Bear, and Dog practice] *Can you two try that again?* [Both Bear and Dog breathe and blow] *Yes, very good belly breaths!"* [Bear and Dog are calmer]

Teacher: *"Bear, you can also come and ask me for help. You can say, 'I want the toy Dog has.' We'll ask Dog to let you have it when he is finished. I will help you wait for your turn. Okay, it looks like Bear feels better and Dog feels better, too. Let's go play!"*

such as biting that always happens at a certain time of day or during a certain activity. These can be important clues to your child's behavior. I provide a blank Injury Report form for your use on page 118. Also included is an Incident Report form for documenting *biting incident attempts* (where there is no victim, thankfully). You may find helpful clues through reviewing patterns associated with attempts to bite.

Action Plan

After you have studied the Seven Questions and any available Injury and/or Incident reports, you will use the Action Plan worksheet to outline changes that are needed to stop the biting. We'll talk more about how to develop the Action Plan later. Just remember that as long as adults agree on the goals and the techniques to reach them, your child will be surrounded by a powerful support system as he or she learns new skills and stops biting.

Part II

Demystify Misbehavior with the Seven Questions

Question 1

How Much of the Child's Behavior Is Related to Typical Social/Emotional Development?

Biting is common among toddlers, twos, and threes. So that you may understand why, our first question deals with typical early childhood development. This chapter provides an overview of the kinds of social/emotional capabilities of these young children. It is important to keep normal development in mind while you consider the roots of a child's biting. Your developmental observations of the child who bites will help you create an Action Plan later.

Toddlers: 12 – 24 months old

Overview
While a toddler is gradually becoming better able to understand another person's likes, dislikes, and feelings, his own personal point of view is still intense. You may notice your toddler exhibiting a strong desire for independence in one situation, then becoming clingy, passive, and completely dependent moments later. He bounces between both feelings on a daily basis. And, while enamored with expanded physical skills that allow him so much mobility, he is still in the process of learning where the boundaries or limits are set in terms of safety. He may refuse to hold an adult's hand and dart into the street. Or he may push a chair up to the counter to get the cookies on the top of the refrigerator, not understanding the danger of falling.

A toddler can get swept up in his strong feelings and need help from an adult to get back to a calm state. He sometimes needs to lean on you as a protector or interpreter for what he is feeling. At other times, he screams "Me do it," demanding full control over the situation. That's part of the daily push–pull of living or working with a toddler; it's tough sledding.

How toddlers play
Toddlers use a simple type of pretend play with objects and roles. They may pretend to drink from an empty cup or to pour milk from an empty pitcher. How they play often depends on the available materials and the encouragement they receive from adults.

Toddlers who exhibit a higher amount of pretend play tend to be more empathetic. And as they develop their own sense of identity, they learn that possessions are separate from themselves.

Sharing, beginning to learn

In toddlerhood, grabbing is rampant and the word "Mine!" resonates in any typical toddler group. They don't understand that "sharing" a possession doesn't mean "surrendering it for good." They seem to believe they have lost an item forever, not just temporarily. They don't understand that they retain ownership while sharing their toys. They go into a panic about this on a regular basis. Positive and enjoyable play experiences with other children facilitated by caring and skillful adults will help toddlers gradually feel more comfortable in sharing toys with others.

Empathy, beginning to develop

Empathy is a concept that children begin developing slowly as toddlers. Though they find it difficult to comprehend or care what anyone else is experiencing, they assume that everyone else can see, hear, and feel their experiences. As a result, they can become frustrated very quickly when people don't rush to meet their needs. This self-centered point of view makes it difficult for toddlers to inhibit impulses, wait patiently, take turns, or share. An undue amount of frustration can lead to aggressive behavior such as biting, grabbing, or hitting.

Tantrums, beginning to separate from parents

Temper tantrums begin in toddlerhood, taking many adults by surprise. Most adults expect a grace period until a child turns two years old. The label "terrible twos" is something of a misnomer because so many children begin the stage of pulling away at about eighteen months, throwing many parents for a loop. At times, a toddler will become distraught, and it is impossible to decipher what set him off. Even with the best powers of detective-like thinking, you may not be able to identify the root cause of the distress.

Cause and effect of behavior

Toddlers are fascinated with cause and effect. Since infancy, they have studied the concept by watching the humans around them and by using a multitude of items. They see parents bring them food when they are hungry or pick up items they throw from the high chair. They play with toys that reward the push of a button with an interesting sound or action. Toddlers have observed that their behaviors promote positive or negative outcomes. When they get what they want, they are more likely to repeat that behavior. In terms of social behavior, when a toddler is allowed to play with a toy he just grabbed from an older sibling, he sees it as one more example of cause and effect. He will understandably become confused and angry when he gets in trouble for doing that same thing in another setting with other children.

Exploring, everything into the mouth

Oral experiences are a big part of how toddlers explore their world. Over a period of many months everything seems to gravitate towards the mouth for a complete sensory investigation. Sometimes toddlers bite people out of the sheer excitement of the moment.

It's as if they can't contain themselves, so they react orally. Also, biting may serve to relieve the tension that builds up in clenched jaws during periods of teething or emotional confusion.

Affectionate biting

Very young toddlers are in the process of learning how to understand the actions of others and to modulate their own actions. For example, when toddlers see other people put their mouths on each other they don't necessarily understand the mechanics of what is going on in there—it is hidden! Sometimes toddler kissing can turn into biting in an otherwise innocent expression of affection. Responding to this kind of bite should be done without too much drama. It generally won't happen again once a clear boundary has been defined for them.

Two-year-olds

Overview

Two-year-olds like routines and rituals and may become quite upset at changes that take them by surprise. They appreciate clear and understandable boundaries and feel most secure with adults who provide this with love, smiles, hugs, and attention. When they don't receive enough positive attention, they may seek out negative attention through using hurtful behaviors. Children of this age are becoming more aware of and can verbalize feelings more often than toddlers.

How twos play

Parallel play is common with children of this age. They enjoy watching others play but are still not adept at sharing, waiting, or taking turns. They still have very little self-control at twenty-four months of age. During the course of the year, self-control increases and two-year-olds begin to enjoy group activities.

Twos are just beginning to show true cooperation in play and empathy toward others. For example, when a peer is hurt or sad, a two may offer help by giving the hurt child a favorite object or a hug.

Children at this age enjoy helping adults with simple tasks, even as they assert their own independence. They may not appreciate being directed in a certain way, and "I do it" is a standard two-year-old expression.

Three-year-olds

Overview

Three-year-olds are generally cooperative and provoke fewer power struggles. Conflicts of all types are less frequent. They are capable of waiting for things longer, delaying gratification. They are extremely curious about the world and more willing to take direction from adults than they were six months earlier.

Threes are typically interested in their peers and able to handle more sophisticated play than twos. While most children of this age often have developed a set of social/emotional skills that help them deal with stressful situations, some will still have a difficult time with impulse control under stress and can easily get overwhelmed. Even though they seem to understand the concept of sharing and turn-taking, they are not always willing to do so. They often still engage in parallel play, playing next to other children but not with them. They enjoy talking to themselves, tend to laugh frequently, and ask lots of questions.

Even though three-year-olds are beginning to play cooperatively, they are not immune from emotional outbursts and intense temper tantrums. Tantrums can still be very loud, full of name calling, kicking, and screaming. Threes can become defensive over toys and possessions, grabbing a toy from someone, striking out to hurt, or hiding toys from others.

How to Help Toddlers

Help children experience consequences of their actions

- Provide young toddlers with plenty of cause-and-effect toys, where the child can make something happen. Good choices include toys with flaps, dials, and knobs.

- Capitalize on a young child's natural interest in cause and effect. Use the "when—then" technique to illustrate how positive behaviors can promote positive outcomes. Say, "*When* we get your coat on, *then* we can open up the door and go outside to play." Or, "*When* you sit down, *then* I will give you a cracker." Or, "*When* Paul puts the truck down, *then* you can pick it up and have a turn with it."

Recognize children's need to put things in their mouths

- Have a good supply of teething toys on hand, ones that children are allowed to put in their mouths. In group care, be sure you pick them up after children set them down. Put them directly into a soap and water bath, then spray with a water and bleach solution (one part bleach to ten parts water). Let the toys air dry.

- Use a diaper pin to attach a favorite teething toy tied to a very short ribbon (to prevent choking) on the child who bites so that it is always handy in an emergency. Encourage the biting child to "put all her bites" on this toy when tension builds.

- Keep a damp washcloth in the refrigerator. Offer it to the toddler during the day when he appears to be cranky due to teething pain. Encourage the toddler to "put all his bites" on this washcloth when necessary.

Give clear choices

- Avoid giving choices to a toddler that you aren't prepared to grant. Don't pose the question, "Time for your bath now, okay?" If the child says, "No!" he is simply exercising the choice you offered. It may be best to actually strike the word *okay* from your vocabulary for a while so you aren't tempted to offer choices inadvertently.

- Look for opportunities to empower the child with decision making. When possible, give a choice between two things when selecting clothing, food, drink, or books.

Promote empathy and turn-taking

- Promote empathy. Say, "I see a little baby crying in his stroller over there. He looks sad. Do you think he might be hungry for lunch?" Or "See how your nanny is smiling? I think she is feeling very happy to see you!"

- Provide opportunities for the child to take care of other living things by helping to water the plants, brush the dog, comfort the baby, or feed the fish.

- Practice taking turns using concrete items that go back and forth visibly. Sit on the floor with the child and roll cars or balls between you as you chant, "Your turn . . . my turn . . . "

- Model how to politely ask for a turn, including what to do while waiting for a turn. "Honey, may I use the hairbrush after you? Thanks. While I'm waiting for my turn I will brush my teeth."

Encourage use of a "lovey"

- Encourage toddlers to use a soft, personal item for self-comforting when upset. If they don't have one, pick one out and encourage them to use it as their new "lovey." Typical loveys are a small soft blanket, a stuffed animal, or even an article of a parent's clothing.

Be reasonable and consistent

- Maintain consistency and reasonable limits. Become a good student of typical developmental abilities for each age so that your expectations are reasonable. Be willing to make adjustments in the way you enforce limits if you find that you have misunderstood your child's abilities. The chapter on limit setting (page 70) will provide more information on this topic.

- Don't allow younger children to grab toys from older children, as in, "Oh, just let the baby have it." Grabbing behavior isn't cute or funny and will lead to bad habits and confusion when it doesn't work with peers and the child is scolded by adults. Be careful not to grab the toy yourself in order to return it to the older child. Model how you want your child to get his or her toy back.

How to Help Two-Year-Olds

Promote empathy, turn-taking, and sharing

- Promote empathy when reading stories aloud. Highlight the perspectives of the characters' feelings. Say, "Rover was excited to go for a walk, wasn't he?" or "I bet Mia felt angry when Jamal knocked over her tower. That must have been hard for her."

- Provide opportunities for the child to take care of other living things by helping to water the lawn, put out crumbs for the birds, dress the baby, or feed the hamster.

- Let your child protect favorite toys from other children by storing them away during play dates. This stage is not the time for insisting she share her most treasured items.

- Provide a large mirror in which the child can look at her whole body. This helps her to learn where her body boundaries are in relation to other people and objects.

Set up routines and schedules

- Help the two-year-old learn patience and understanding of the passage of time by maintaining a routine as much as possible. In conversations, mention what happened recently, what is currently happening, and what is about to happen next. Help the child to see the pattern in the day. Providing a chart with pictures can help children visualize progressive events and lessen the frustration of the unknown.

- Be mindful of how long you expect the child to comfortably wait for things. Suggest ways for her to occupy herself while waiting. Have a note pad on hand for drawing or a travel game to play while waiting. Fingerplay songs are also useful at these times.

How to Help Three-Year-Olds

Promote turn-taking

- Play simple games that involve taking turns, such as picture matching and lotto games.

- Describe what you see, as in, "I see two angry children. It seems like both you and Latisha want a turn with the bike at the same time."

- When you see a child put a toy down, ask him if he is "done with his turn." Help him to understand that by leaving the item, he has made the decision to allow someone else to take the next "new turn." He can't expect the toy to be safe from use by someone else.

- Point out times that you have to wait for turns. At the meat counter say, "Let's pull a ticket number so we can get ready for our turn. We can watch the numbers to see our turn get closer. Even grown-ups have to take turns."

Help children understand feelings and develop control over actions

- Use music to play games of stopping and starting and to promote enjoyable experiences in gaining better control of actions.

■ Offer physical activities that help children deal with strong feelings in an appropriate way: drums, play dough, shovels for digging, paper tearing, balls to throw, large sheets of paper for painting, etc.

■ Use active listening when children are upset so they know you understand what they are feeling. Say, "I can see how mad you are that you can't get that puzzle piece to fit."

Set up routines and schedules

■ Predictable routines help children know what to expect, help them "tell time," and lessen anxiety. For example, dinner, then bath, then story means it's almost time for bed.

■ Abrupt changes in the day can cause anger and outbursts in young children. Try to provide your child with an advance warning five or ten minutes before a change in activities so he doesn't have to shift gears too fast.

■ Provide options and choices whenever possible to reduce power struggles by sharing the power. Say, "Do you want to put your pajamas on before or after the story?"

Action Review 1

Question 1: *How much of the child's behavior is related to typical social/emotional development?*

Put a check in the boxes of any actions that you think might help the biting child. In Part IV, you will refer to this list as you fill out an Action Plan worksheet.

❑ Help the child understand consequences of actions.
Notes: _____

_____

❑ Recognize the need for oral expression.
Notes: _____

_____

❑ Offer clear choices.
Notes: _____

_____

❑ Promote empathy, turn-taking, and sharing.
Notes: _____

_____

❑ Encourage use of a lovey.
Notes: _____

_____

❑ Be reasonable and consistent in your expectations.
Notes: _____

_____

❑ Establish routines and schedules.
Notes: _____

_____

❑ Help the child understand feelings and develop control of actions.
Notes: _____

_____

❑ What else might you want to consider to help this child?
Notes: _____

_____

Question 2

What Past Experiences or Recent Changes May Be Creating Stress?

Experience affects human behavior. Another path to the root of any behavior problem is the child's personal experiences. They may provide clues as to what is causing the child to act out, filling in some of the missing puzzle pieces. Knowing more about the child's past experiences and recent changes will help you design meaningful, lasting solutions for the future.

Reviewing the past and present openly

To begin developing a successful solution to a biting problem, parents and caregivers will have an honest and open discussion where they each share relevant details of the child's previous experiences around or with hurtful behavior. Without this background information, parents and caregivers will be working under a handicap. For example, has the child been around siblings, cousins, or neighbors at home who act out in hurtful ways? Has there been aggressive behavior at the fitness center child care room or religious day program? Does anyone play biting games with the child?

Parents' information about the child who bites

Parents need to be up-front and honest about previous troublesome experiences with the child's caregiver or teacher. Admittedly, this can be embarrassing, especially if parents have kept this information under wraps thus far. They should describe the times of day that the biting occurred at the other program or at home and how adults responded to the incidents. It may be that an adult's reactions to the behavior confused the child and intensified the problem. Knowing as much as possible about how the situation was handled, or even just what the child was exposed to, will help adults know what kinds of actions to emphasize or what kinds

> Ethan, 18 months old, sat in a circle outside on the playground, waiting for afternoon snacks to be passed out by the caregivers. He calmly leaned over to the little girl on his left, mouth partly open, and quickly bit her on the shoulder in an apparent preemptive strike, as if to say, "You are simply too close for my comfort."

Chris, 18 months old, attempted to bite children at the infant/toddler center on a daily basis. He was getting mixed messages about his behavior. At the center, he was reprimanded, but at home his dad routinely played biting games with him. ("You're so yummy. Watch out, Chris, I am going to come eat you up.") Chris was also encouraged to engage in rough play with the family dog, entertaining his parents who howled with laughter.

of damage control to activate.

Caregivers should share with parents any relevant past experiences in the program that may have affected the child. Talking openly about the past hurtful experiences within the group creates a collaborative atmosphere. It puts everyone on the same playing field while working on solving the problem. Review together any written Injury Reports that are available from prior hurtful situations.

When the child has been a victim of biting or other hurtful behavior in the past, it is useful to discuss the dynamics of who was involved and how it was managed. This can help clarify how the child has interpreted and internalized the situation. The victim may have concluded that biting is a good preemptive action for protecting oneself against future harm. She may have been impressed by seeing how other children gained center stage while hurting others, even if all they gained was negative attention.

Parents' biting as a form of play

Some adults play rough, physical games with young children, or use biting in what they think is a harmless, playful manner. They lean down and nibble at their child's toes or tummy during a clothing change, pretending to be an alligator or a friendly monster, saying, "I'm going to eat you up, oh yes I am!" They laugh and laugh while doing this, encouraging the child to laugh and play along. Though meant in good fun, the child is receiving confusing messages. On the one hand, biting is perceived as a playful romp; at other times, the child is disciplined for putting his teeth on people, even if he meant no harm but just got carried away in the excitement. Biting games can create a great deal of confusion for children. It's better to stop them altogether.

Changes or stressors in a child's life

Life is full of surprises. Some are happy ones; others we can do without. When living through a time of crisis, particularly one that is unexpected, it can take all of our emotional resources to maintain some semblance of normalcy, order, and routine within our family.

When children are overwhelmed by stress they may act out or misbehave. Supporting children through these tough times is crucial. If they can learn to cope, children will develop confidence and new competencies, becoming resilient and stronger in the process.

Examples of stressors for young children

Following are two lists of the kinds of stressors that can provoke anxiety in very young children. These situations are normal occurrences that happen to many families, and, while difficult, they need to be dealt with in thoughtful and compassionate ways for the benefit of all.

Within the family:
Parent gone due to travel, deployment, or
hospitalization
Tension between family members
Birth of a sibling
Moving to a new home
Changing to a new bedroom
Divorce or separation of parents
Unemployment
Death of a pet or family member
Holidays—even happy occasions create
changes to routine
Out of town guests—having to share
parents with others

Within the child development program:
Absence of a favorite teacher
Introduction of a new teacher or caregiver
Absence of a favorite friend
Increased hours of child care
Moving to a new classroom or child care
setting with new procedures
and new rules
Going from a crib to a nap mat

> Jasmine, 18 months old, exhibited new behaviors such as whining, fussing, and trying to bite children at every play group gathering. Any kind of minor frustration with others would trigger a biting attempt. On the home front, the family was going through some big changes. Mom was preparing for a major professional exam and was suffering severe jaw joint problems from clenching her teeth due to the stress. Dad was working extra long hours, coming home depleted and uncommunicative after his long train ride. At the end of the day, neither parent had enough emotional reserves left for Jasmine. The tension felt by her parents had now affected her, too.

Signs of stress

Usually, there are some telltale signs of heightened anxiety when children are overtaxed with stress, but these signs may be subtle and unique to each child. They may include: an increase in whining, a shorter than average fuse, becoming flushed and flustered, withdrawal, increased stuttering, twirling or pulling hair, or increased sucking on fingers or thumb. These types of behaviors may be normal for some children and are usually expressed mildly. For others, these behaviors are new and may be early warning signs, a call for compassionate and sensitive handling. When adults don't respond to early signs of anxiety, the behavior may escalate into agitation and a loss of control, including impulsiveness, tantrums, hitting, and biting.

How to Help the Child

Understand his or her past experiences

- Stop playing biting games with the child and make sure others do so as well, explaining why it is confusing to the child.

- Review the child care program's existing Injury Report form to make sure it is comprehensive enough and allows enough room on the page for adequate reporting. (See Appendix I for sample Injury and Incident Report forms.)

- Review all completed Injury and Incident reports regarding the child, looking for patterns in terms of time of day, location, etc. You will utilize this data when you create your Action Plan.

Get professional help for your marriage or other significant relationship

- Parents who are in a troubled marriage or relationship should go to a marriage counselor to work out the issues in a facilitated manner, gaining new insights and tools for success.

- Avoid arguing with other family members in the presence of children. Find private times to discuss volatile issues. Raised voices and out-of-control actions frighten and confuse children.

Don't disappear from the house

- When you leave the house, leave with a positive attitude and calm demeanor so as not to alarm the child and cause anxiety. Children can be frightened when adults disappear unexpectedly.

Give child forewarning of changes

- Give the child as much notice as possible if you have to change her routine in any way. For example, if she expects Daddy to pick her up from child care but Aunt Emily has to do it for him, tell her ahead of time. Then call, prior to the pick-up, to have the caregiver remind the child.

- Talk about any significant upcoming changes in the daily life of the child a few days ahead of time, during a period when you have enough time to sensitively manage the child's emotional reaction. Bring it up at a time when you are not rushed or stressed or on the run. Use active listening to respond while staying optimistic about the outcome. ("I know that is not what you are used to, and it feels confusing to you, but everything will be all right.")

Connect with child during absences

- When a parent is traveling or hospitalized, use a calendar to count down the days until the loved one will be home. Have photos handy and have the child and parent talk by phone or the Internet frequently.

- Before a planned absence, record some audio tapes of yourself reading stories to your child. At the appropriate times, say, "Now turn the page." While you are away, she can listen to the tapes and look at the book just as though you were there together.

Take time with grief and reflection

- When a loved one dies, even a pet, children may be upset for quite a while.

They often believe that the loved one will come back to them eventually. Help them to understand the permanence of the situation by commenting on the finality of other things that have died, when you see that happen in your daily life. Say, "Looks like the flowers have finished blooming and are dead now. I'm glad we were able to appreciate them while they were here. They had such a beautiful life. Time to put them away now."

■ Use children's picture books that deal with the topic of death in a sensitive way.

Carve out private time together

■ When a new baby comes home, be proactive in finding ways to spend private time with your older child. At first, he may not understand that the baby is here to stay. Many children truly believe that the baby is visiting and will be returned to the hospital eventually. Your older child needs to be reassured of your love for him in very concrete ways. Let him do some special household activities with you that only "big kids" can do, such as mixing up pancakes, pouring the orange juice, dusting the coffee table, etc.

Provide outlets for intense feelings

■ Steer an upset child toward activities that can help her work out her feelings in a physical yet constructive way. Provide play dough, clay, plastic bats, paints with big brushes, or shovels for digging, so children can channel that energy in an appropriate way.

■ Provide soft music, stuffed animals, puppets, pillows, flannel boards, etc., for creating peaceful nooks and crannies, quiet places from which to draw comfort.

Use active listening

■ Use active listening to paraphrase feelings that a child exhibits. For example, "You seem worried about someone taking your blanket. Is that right?" See Appendix III for more examples.

Action Review 2

Question 2: *What past experiences or recent changes may be creating stress?*

Put a check in the boxes of any actions that you think might help the biting child. In Part IV, you will refer to this list as you fill out an Action Plan worksheet.

❏ Discuss past incidents with parents and caregivers and look for themes.

Notes: _____

_____

❏ Record at home or in a group setting the details of each aggressive behavior incident using a comprehensive Injury or Incident Report form.

Notes: _____

_____

❏ Stop playing biting games.

Notes: _____

_____

❏ Get family counseling; stop arguing in front of the child.

Notes: _____

_____

❏ Tell the child when you are leaving; don't suddenly disappear.

Notes: _____

_____

❏ Give the child advance notice of changes.

Notes: _____

_____

❏ Stay connected to the child while absent.

Notes: _____

_____

❏ Take grief and reflection slowly.

Notes: _____

_____

❏ Carve out enough private time with the child.

Notes: _____

_____

❏ Provide the child with outlets for intense feelings.

Notes: _____

_____

❏ Use active listening.

Notes: _____

_____

❏ What else might you want to consider to help this child?

Notes: _____

_____

Question 3

Is the Lack of Verbal Skills Causing Frustration?

This chapter focuses on how to support language development, to give children a good base from which to build specific social skills. There are many concrete things people can do to help a child communicate. A key to success is modeling verbal expressions for children during these potent developmental stages. Being able to express oneself in words can go a long way in stopping biting behavior.

Speech and language development is a continuous process that involves every aspect of the individual— intellectual, motor, emotional, and social. Most children have produced their first word by the age of twelve months. By the time he or she enters kindergarten, that same child will likely know more than 14,000 words. Some children, particularly those with special needs or certain types of learning challenges, may be on a different time line.

Learning how to talk

While children have an inborn capacity for language acquisition, learning to use language does not occur on its own. Children don't learn to communicate by watching television. *They learn through interactions with live humans.* Furthermore, conversations between adults and children teach language skills better than conversations between children. Why? Because adults are more adept at interpreting, defining, verbally probing, and supplying words until they get the full meaning of the child's message. Generally, in conversations between children, the listener (another child) is not as skilled or patient in reading between the lines of the child's words as an adult. The child listener has little to offer in the way of interpretive help to the child speaker, so it is no wonder that misunderstandings and frustration are a common outcome of

Randy, 17 months old, had begun to bite other children in his class, sometimes making twenty biting attempts per day! His hearing seemed fine and he was making two- and three-word sentences, but he never used language with the other children when becoming frustrated. He simply tried to bite them. At home, Randy's mom used mostly baby-talk with Randy. She admitted to not setting any limits on his behavior because she "didn't want to make him mad at her." She also worried about replicating the negative childhood she had experienced as a young girl. As a result, she was permissive and lenient, treating Randy like a baby and never allowing him to become frustrated at home. These factors prevented Randy from learning to use language to help curb his impulses when frustrated in class.

these interactions, with hurtful behavior often following close behind.

Adults can lower frustration levels and increase language skills by speaking to children in ways that help them interpret the actions of other people. By modeling positive communication skills, you increase children's ability to get along with others.

Speech and language

Speech is produced by many muscular movements. For example, take the one-syllable word *church*. Speaking that one word involves twenty different adjustments of the lips, tongue, larynx, and jaws. These adjustments must be made precisely and in correct sequence. According to experts, the word requires less than a quarter of a second to say, so the average time available for each of the necessary movements is 100th of a second. Most people are very surprised at this close relationship between motor development and speech.

Language is a broader category than speech and refers to any means, vocal or otherwise, of expressing or understanding feelings or thought. Children, like adults, use language to translate or control a situation, label something, locate or call attention to something, identify ownership, control something, share a point of view, or play with words.

Speech and language milestones

At 12–18 months
A child can typically string together two-syllable words such as Mama, Dada, and Baba. Wants and needs are indicated with a word, gesture, or vocalization. She can obey simple commands such as "come here" or "open your mouth." She will retrieve something upon request, such as a toy or a shoe. She will absentmindedly vocalize a variety of sounds and words for fun, a practice called *echolalia*. She will develop true speech and language comprehension and begin to use single words meaningfully. Most children will have spoken a few words by the age of 15 months and will enjoy trying to name familiar objects. When she says the word "ball" she may mean "Where is the ball?" or "I see a ball" or "Give me the ball." Toddlers expect the adults around them to interpret their meanings with very few word clues, a challenge for parents and caregivers.

At 18 months
A child can typically say twenty to thirty words, although some say less while others can say up to fifty words by this age. Speech includes nouns, verbs, and powerful words like "mine," "no," "fast," and "more." She likes to mix words together that have no meaning, playing with the actions and sounds of forming speech. This type of speech is called jargon, and it is the practice of fluency. She can also point to things that are named, such as "ball," "dog," "nose," "feet," and "mouth." At this age, she is a word collector and she enjoys imitating the sounds of animals. She may refer to herself by name rather than by a pronoun, saying, "Amy do it." She is beginning to make two- and three-word sentences. She expects to be understood, though, even when her speech is unclear to others.

At two years
A two-year-old can typically say between twenty to 300 words. Her speech now includes verbs, pronouns, and adjectives. She is learning the rules of language, such as "big dog"

instead of "dog big" and when to make a word plural or past tense. She enjoys songs and rhymes and talks to herself during play, often saying the same thing over and over. Most children in this age group do not yet have fluent articulation and may be missing sounds at the middle and ends of many words. They will be about 50% intelligible and may be using three-word sentences. There is typically some *dysfluency* at this age, stuttering or a broken rhythm, and the voice may not be well modulated, sometimes being too loud or too soft.

At three years

By three years, a child can typically communicate with between 600 to 1,000 words in up to four-word sentences. She is using full sentences in the right context to get what she wants or to express an idea and can even grasp nuances in complex words such as slippery, worried, excited, etc. She adds many descriptive words to her own speech such as favorite, best, tallest, etc., and will use them over and over. She can follow a two-part direction, such as "Please go to the counter and get your cup of juice." She will still be confused, however, by slang or words that have more than one meaning.

Is something wrong with the child's language development?

Sometimes, even with the best modeling and communication techniques, a child does not make significant progress in language development. When that happens it is best for parents to investigate further using professional guidance. Some common reasons for speech and language delays are hearing loss, developmental challenges, or oral muscular difficulties.

Hearing problems

It may be that the child has a hearing problem related to past ear infections. Children who have frequent ear infections do not hear sounds consistently and may have trouble in learning to speak and to understand the conversations of people around them. This can lead to a high degree of frustration, which can lead to hurtful behavior under stress. Research shows a correlation between ear infections and delayed speech and language. While battling an ear infection, children often have a significant temporary hearing loss that can impact their language development.

Developmental problems

A speech and language delay may also be related to a developmental problem such as autism or a learning disorder. Either is best determined by a therapeutic team assessment.

Some children have trouble chewing food and forming words due to inadequate muscle control or a structural abnormality in the mouth. A licensed speech and language therapist can make that determination and provide the appropriate intervention. If any of the following situations are true for your child, you should seek an evaluation with a licensed speech and language therapist.

> Cameron, age 3, had limited speech that was very hard to understand, though he seemed to comprehend everything said to him. He had been evaluated at age 2 and found to be developmentally delayed in speech and language. Frustrated at trying to get the adults around him to understand him, he would run at his parents and bite their thighs. His biting and their bruises decreased as his ability to make himself understood increased.

Speech and language red flags:

Before her first birthday, the child does not babble, vocalize, or gesture.

By the age of sixteen months, the child has not said her first word.

By her second birthday, the child has not said a two-word phrase.

By two and a half years, the child is not putting two- to three-word sentences together.

At three years, the child is unintelligible by family and friends more than half the time.

At any age, the child shows a loss of previously exhibited language skills.

How to Help the Child

Provide words

■ Elaborate on the child's short phrases. For example, when a child points to the fruit bowl and says, "Manana," hand her the banana saying, "It sounds like you are hungry for a big, yellow banana." Using this *extension* technique honors the child's attempt at communication while modeling more sophisticated language skills. Refrain from asking her to repeat your extensions. Just let her hear you use them in the proper context.

Be a commentator

■ Act as a commentator on children's activities, similar to the sportscaster at an athletic event. Hearing someone describe what is going on helps children see their place within the group as just one part of the whole picture. They hear someone mention some of the "play choices" that are currently available "on the field." Acting as a neutral and friendly commentator is different than giving directives. It is simply an overlay that describes what you see; it is not meant to be a veil for manipulation. Use phrases such as *"I see that . . ."* to help children decipher the situation-at-hand. *"I see that* Brianna is building a tall tower with all of the red blocks right now."* Comment on pro-social behavior approvingly by saying, *"I see* John and Pablo taking turns using the big sand shovel. Nice digging, boys."*

Describe your own actions

■ Use self-talk to describe your actions and purpose. Say, "I'm scooping out the paste, reaching way down into the jar" or "This sand is causing people to slip; I'll sweep it out of the way." This kind of communication models how sentences are put together.

Use starter phrases

■ Use starter phrases such as *"I have an idea . . . "* as an effective, nonthreatening way to get a child's attention. "I have an idea for you . . . listen, let's take the riding toy over to the floor where there is more room." This phrase acts like a signal, an interactional buffer. It peaks the child's interest in what you are about to say. He has a chance to ready himself for the coming suggestion rather than getting caught off guard. Since you haven't started off with a directive, such as "Randy, quit banging into the table," you have not set yourself up for a power struggle.

Say, "I wonder . . ."

- Model thoughtfulness and a sense of wonder by demonstratively pausing for thought. Use the phrase, *"I wonder . . ."* on a regular basis to demonstrate how people can think before reacting. For example, *"I wonder* if Marco is almost ready to get out of the bathtub?" or *"I wonder* what it would look like if I cut the sandwich into triangles instead of squares?" or *"I wonder* when Maggie will be done with her turn on the swing?" Help children to see that it isn't necessary to have all the answers.

Be patient

- Give your child enough time to complete her thoughts. It may take her extra time to put what she wants to say into words. Do not rush her. You may even have to repeat your remark so that she can hear it again, *giving her more time to process what you have said.*

Read to your child

- Read aloud to children as much as possible. Talk to your librarian to find books appropriate for their developmental level that focus on social/emotional topics.

Action Review 3

Question 3: *Is the lack of verbal skills causing frustration?*

Put a check in the boxes of any actions that you think might help the biting child. In Part IV, you will refer to this list as you fill out an Action Plan worksheet.

❏ Extend the child's language; provide words.

Notes: _____

_____

❏ Be a commentator.

Notes: _____

_____

❏ Use self-talk; describe your thoughts and actions aloud.

Notes: _____

_____

❏ Use starter phrases.

Notes: _____

_____

❏ Model thoughtfulness and wonder.

Notes: _____

_____

❏ Be patient while the child talks.

Notes: _____

_____

❏ Read to the child.

Notes: _____

_____

❏ What else might you want to consider to help this child?

Notes: _____

_____

Question 4

Is the Child's Physical Condition a Contributing Factor?

Sickness, hunger, fatigue, and other physical conditions can definitely be a cause of stress for young children. Sometimes adults can intervene in helpful ways, such as better management of a hungry child or cold items offered to a teething toddler. Of course, children who are frequently irritable or strike out at others should be seen by a pediatrician to treat or rule out ear infections, allergies, or other illness. Observe the child's physical capabilities to see if problems with motor skills are impacting his or her play. It may be necessary to consult with a physical therapist as well as a pediatrician to assess the situation. Consider if these or other physical issues are at the root of the biting.

Physical conditions that lead to irritability

Ear infections
Children who have frequent ear infections do not hear sounds consistently and can have trouble learning to speak and comprehend others around them. This can cause a lack of understanding and be highly frustrating. Also, the actual pain from an undiagnosed ear infection may contribute to the child's biting episodes. Biting on something releases pressure in the ear, leading to reduction of pain.

Teething
Infants begin cutting their front teeth months before their first birthday and toddlers continue to teethe throughout most of their second year of life. Most cut their first and second sets of molars between twelve and twenty-four months, which can cause quite a bit of discomfort. Some children become incredibly irritable during teething and may bite and chew on things to relieve the pain. Sucking on bottles tends to make the pain worse, so it helps to switch from the bottle to the cup during the second year of life. Your doctor may advise using a pain reliever on occasion. Offer the child something cool to bite on from time to time while teething, like a cool, damp washcloth.

Hunger

According to a publication by medical professionals, the *Child Health Alert* newsletter (December 2002), the frequency of biting is often highest in the middle of the morning. This information matches my own observations and many of the incidents reported to me by caregivers or parents. It is likely no coincidence that these biting incidents occurred during the hours between snack time and lunchtime.

At a child care center: Families who use child care are usually up at the crack of dawn. Everyone must be washed, dressed, fed, and dropped off early enough for the parent to get to work on time. Some young children don't like to eat much early in the morning, especially if feeling rushed. And they may be too distracted by classroom activities to eat much during morning snack time, which may be around 9:30 A.M. By the time 10:30 or 11:00 rolls around, they may be famished. Given a typical daily schedule where everyone eats at the same time, lunch is not usually available to the group until closer to noon. Also, it is not unusual during this period of the late morning for children to be brought outside while a caregiver places nap cots down on the floor inside. Other caregivers rotate on and off the playground, taking their once-per-morning fifteen-minute break.

These factors can become the perfect storm for hurtful behavior to occur: hunger and fatigue can play a big role in a child's lack of self-control. In a child care center, there are often fewer adults "on the floor" per child during that morning period. Also, if the play area is too small for the group and/or lacking in appropriate items, well . . . hurtful behavior may not be far behind.

At home: The same problem with hunger can be true in a home setting. Children may be out with family members or with a nanny, running errands or on a play date. The closer it gets to lunchtime, the bigger the chance these children will fall apart emotionally. You can watch their behavior deteriorate until they act out uncontrollably. Toddlers and two-year-olds don't know how to recognize their feelings of depletion as hunger. They may not know to ask for food until they are out of control. This awareness will come later as they grow into preschoolers.

Distractions to eating

Clearly, some children are less interested in food than others. They are harder to get to the table than those who love to eat. Many children get so engrossed in their play that they resist being stopped, even to refuel. When they do suddenly run out of gas, they can get cranky and sometimes even aggressive with other children. Those with the strong "irregularity" trait in their temperament (see Question 5) make it especially difficult for their parents and caregivers to identify their needs in this area. These children are often hard to "read," making it tough to predict when they will run out of steam and finally be ready to eat.

Lack of sleep

When hurtful behavior occurs in the late afternoon, there's a good chance the child is low on emotional resources due to nighttime sleep problems or truncated or missed naps. Rapidly growing young children need a great deal of time to refresh their bodies through sleep. Twelve- to-eighteen-month-olds typically sleep 11.5–15.5 hours per day, including naps. Children between eighteen and thirty months typically sleep 11–14 hours per day, including naps. Three-year-olds need about 10.5–14 hours of sleep per day. Toddlers and twos rarely skip naps by choice. They usually exhaust themselves with constant physical activity and are more than ready for an afternoon nap. At night, they should be sleeping independently and soundly.

Sleep interruption

Circumstances sometimes demand that adults interrupt a child's normal sleep routine. At other times, adults can change their plans, that is, cancel a car trip or cut play time short to accommodate a tired child. That may be tough to accomplish when caring for children of various ages and needs. For example, some parents have no choice but to roust their two-year-old from a nap in order to pick up an older sibling at school. If a situation demands interrupting a child's sleep, be aware that you are putting the child at a disadvantage and you should expect struggles due to fatigue.

Forcing a child to skip naps

Some parents mistakenly believe that a young child who naps will have difficulty falling asleep at night. In fact, no nap can instead produce an overtired child who either can't fall asleep at night or who sleeps fitfully. While parents may want to get their child to bed early, keeping a tired and cranky child awake in the afternoon to accomplish this goal is counterproductive. Better to get the child on a schedule that includes a daily early afternoon nap or quiet time so the child can recharge her batteries and go into the evening with enough resources to be content rather than fussy.

Motor problems

Some toddlers and twos have trouble coordinating their movements and feel especially vulnerable during periods of very active play. This can be due to undiagnosed problems with physical growth and motor skills. They may use biting as a form of self-protection, feeling nervous about being knocked over by more active children. For example, if you are wondering why your child is aggressive around other children, complains about walking, falls often, and frequently asks to be carried, take a closer look at how he or she moves. If the child's physical movements appear awkward or stilted, talk with your pediatrician. Also talk to a specialist in this area, such as a physical or occupational therapist. If a physical problem is discovered, therapeutic services can be started before the child turns three years old, providing vital intervention at an early age.

Two-year-old Spencer had been biting his classmates for several months, most often in the gross motor playroom, where children were freer to run, jump, slide, dance, use riding toys and balls, etc. Upon closer observation, it appeared that his large motor skills were not as smooth as they should be for his age; he moved in an uncoordinated manner. He also seemed worried about getting too close to other children. Frequently, he tried to claim the top of the slide, perched safely above the others, often biting those who tried to interfere. Through a diagnostic assessment with a specialist, it was discovered that one leg was slightly shorter than the other, causing him to feel off-balance and more vulnerable around active play.

How to Help the Child

Address all contributing physical conditions

■ Reflect on any physical conditions that may be affecting the child's behavior. Find a way to positively address each issue. Schedule a visit to your pediatrician or specialist if needed.

■ If sleep issues are a persistent problem for your household, do additional research on how best to manage your child's sleep habits. Three excellent sleep resources are *Helping Your Child Sleep Through the Night* by Joanne Cuthbertson and Susie Schevill; *Sleep: The Brazelton Way* by T. Berry Brazelton, M.D., and Joshua D. Sparrow, M.D.; and *The Sleep Book for Tired Parents* by Rebecca Huntley.

■ If hunger issues are evident, look for ways to get more creative in what kinds of food you are offering the child. Young children often respond well to finger food that is colorful and fun to eat. Also, they are more likely to try new things if they can help prepare meals: tearing up lettuce, stirring the pot, pouring milk from a child-sized pitcher, etc. For more ideas, see *Child of Mine: Feeding with Love and Good Sense* by Ellyn Satter.

Create a new daily schedule to lessen fatigue and hunger

■ Consider making some daily schedule changes to better support the child's needs.

■ Structure the day so as to avoid unnecessary overstimulation during the hours when your child becomes most tired. For example, some children benefit from shorter play dates with fewer children. Also, adults can select activities that are most conducive to calm play (see Question 7). Strategies like these can help children manage their energy levels.

Try not to interrupt or skip naps

■ Bring along a comfort item, a lovey, when traveling with a tired child. With its help, the child may be able to nap in unfamiliar places.

■ Do everything in your power to allow your child his or her naptime.

Action Review 4

Question 4: *Is the child's physical condition a contributing factor?*

Put a check in the boxes of any actions that you think might help the biting child. In Part IV, you will refer to this list as you fill out an Action Plan worksheet.

❑ Identify and address physical problems.

Notes: _____

_____

❑ Deal with sleeping and eating issues.

Notes: _____

_____

❑ Seek additional help as needed.

Notes: _____

_____

❑ Lessen fatigue with a well-planned daily schedule.

Notes: _____

_____

❑ Protect naptimes and provide comforting items to induce calm.

Notes: _____

_____

❑ What else might you want to consider to help this child?

Notes: _____

_____

Question 5

What Role Does the Child's Temperament Play in the Behavior?

Each child is unique, responding to events and the environment in a variety of ways. For centuries, people have wondered what causes children to behave in such different ways. How much is influenced by environmental changes and how much is simply "hard-wired" or inborn? How can two siblings be so different, even when they were raised by the same parents, in the same home, with the same toys, etc.? How can a child be so different from his parents? In this chapter we will consider the ways in which a child's temperament may affect his behavior, particularly biting. While temperament research is ongoing, the following information has been found to be very helpful to parents and others who work directly with children.

Defining temperament

Temperament refers to the traits your child is born with; it is her natural, inborn style of responding to events and her environment. Think of it as the "how" of behavior, not the "why." To identify temperament traits, you would ask yourself questions; for example, "How did she act when I tried to change her clothes?" (not "Why did she complain about it?"). Temperament is not produced by the environment and it is not created by parenting—we are born with it. Adults can modify temperament and soften the rough edges, so to speak, but they cannot change it entirely.

According to many of the studies on temperament, each person exhibits varying degrees of nine temperamental traits. The categories are: activity level, regularity, initial reaction to new experiences, adaptability to change, sensory awareness, intensity of expression, general mood, distractibility, and persistence.

While people have many physical, social, and psychological factors in common, their actual behavior may vary dramatically. They may differ in the way they approach a new social situation, the quickness in which they move, the intensity of their emotional expressions, and their distractibility when they are absorbed in an activity. Those are some of the temperament traits that create different styles of behavior.

The goal: goodness of fit

Goodness of fit means that even though children are born with a certain set of traits, situations can deemphasize and soften (creating a goodness of fit), or accentuate and worsen (creating a bad fit) any of the traits. Disturbances, it was found, were more likely to arise when the temperament of the child and the expectations of the adults were out-of-sync. Goodness of fit has to do with compatibility between the child and the environment. The traits themselves are neither good nor bad. What matters is how the environment supports them. Goodness of fit doesn't mean absence of stress, but it does allow the child to more effectively optimize his ability to cope with problems in socially acceptable and emotionally healthy ways.

Adults who understand a child's temperament and adjust their techniques accordingly consistently experience fewer behavior problems with the child. That doesn't mean that they give up on expecting children to learn to cope with things that are difficult for them. It means they have learned to combine firm limit setting with sympathetic, expert management of behavior. These adults identify where the child has the most difficulties, temperamentally speaking, and then adjust the environment, expectations, and management of situations.

Temperament rating scale

Every temperament trait is exhibited by all of us at some level, from high to moderate to low. Here is a rating scale that will help you understand both the child's temperament and your own. The next section of this chapter will provide ideas for sensitive management of situations commonly affected by temperament. Using a pencil, jot down how your child exhibits each trait by putting his or her initials on the rating scale under the description of each trait. Place your own initials on the rating scale, too. You will likely discover that you share some traits with your child, but are far apart on others. Think all the way back to your child's behavior as a baby as you go through the nine traits.

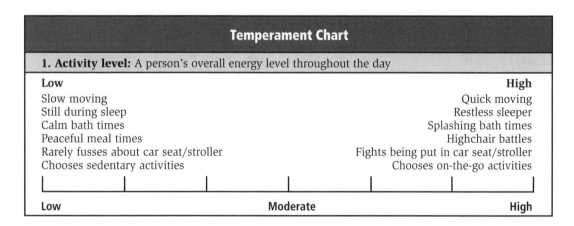

Temperament Chart (continued)

2. Regularity: The day-to-day predictability of hunger, sleep, and elimination.

Hunger
Wants food at the same time of day   Irregular eater
Predictable amounts of food   Difficult to predict appetite

High		**Moderate**			**Low**

Sleep
Tired on schedule   No schedule

High		**Moderate**			**Low**

Elimination
BMs at same time daily   Try and guess

High		**Moderate**			**Low**

3. Withdrawal or Approach: A person's initial tendency for responding to a new experience, new person, or new environment.

Outgoing   Guarded
Eager   Slow to warm up
Adventurous   Cautious

Approach		**Moderate**			**Withdraw**

4. Adaptability to environmental changes: How easily a person handles attempts to influence what he or she is doing or thinking.

Adapts quickly to new routine   Trouble coping with change in routine
Moves easily from two naps to one   Difficulty with change in schedules
Easy-going attitude with changes to   Becomes upset with changes to
  physical setting   environment
Smooth transitions during the day   Transitions cause distress

High		**Moderate**			**Low**

5. Sensory Awareness: How sensitive a person is in each of his/her sensory channels: pain, sight, sound, touch, smell, or taste. How much complaining does a person do regarding noise, lights, room temperature, odors, new tastes, etc.? Do people describe this person as "finicky" or not? Rate each channel separately.

Pain
"EEEEOOOOWWWW"   "What pain in my foot?"

High		**Moderate**			**Low**

Temperament Chart (continued)

Touch

Always aware of the sensation, easily irritated or pleased
Ultra sensitive to tags on clothes or fabric type

No reaction to touch
Doesn't notice

High   **Moderate**   **Low**

Taste

Notices tiny variations; may comment on it
Reacts strongly to certain foods

Can't seem to tell the difference
Generally accepting of new foods

High   **Moderate**   **Low**

Smell

Like a human bloodhound

Doesn't seem to notice odors

High   **Moderate**   **Low**

Hearing/Sound

Sensitive to sounds

Noise often goes unnoticed

High   **Moderate**   **Low**

Sight/Light

Complains about brightness

Doesn't seem bothered by it

High   **Moderate**   **Low**

6. Intensity of Responses: The amount of energy a person commonly uses to express emotions.

Impressive tantrums
Strong reaction to failure
Eats with gusto
Wears his emotions "on his sleeve"
Lots of drama

Mild show of temper
Pouting
Eats carefully
Hard to read
Mild display of emotions

High   **Moderate**   **Low**

7. General Mood or Disposition: The person's predominant mood.

Negative outlook much of the time
Glass is half empty
Pensive, somber look on face
Pessimist

A typically sunny disposition
Glass is half full
Upbeat, cheerful countenance
Optimist

Negative   **Moderate**   **Positive**

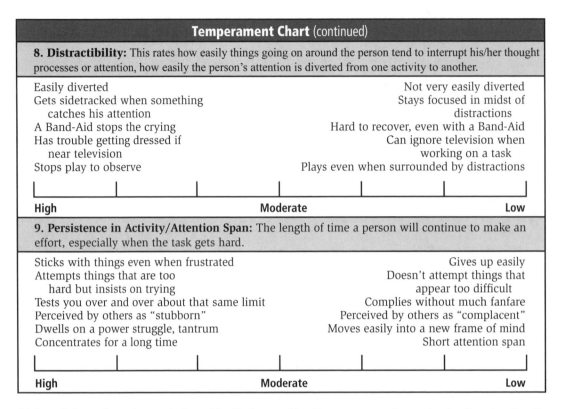

Temperament Chart (continued)

8. Distractibility: This rates how easily things going on around the person tend to interrupt his/her thought processes or attention, how easily the person's attention is diverted from one activity to another.

High	Moderate	Low
Easily diverted		Not very easily diverted
Gets sidetracked when something catches his attention		Stays focused in midst of distractions
A Band-Aid stops the crying		Hard to recover, even with a Band-Aid
Has trouble getting dressed if near television		Can ignore television when working on a task
Stops play to observe		Plays even when surrounded by distractions

9. Persistence in Activity/Attention Span: The length of time a person will continue to make an effort, especially when the task gets hard.

High	Moderate	Low
Sticks with things even when frustrated		Gives up easily
Attempts things that are too hard but insists on trying		Doesn't attempt things that appear too difficult
Tests you over and over about that same limit		Complies without much fanfare
Perceived by others as "stubborn"		Perceived by others as "complacent"
Dwells on a power struggle, tantrum		Moves easily into a new frame of mind
Concentrates for a long time		Short attention span

(Adapted from the rating scale found in *Understanding Temperament: Strategies for Creating Family Harmony* by Lyndall Shick, M.A. Used with permission from Parenting Press.)

Creating a good fit for children

If you are dealing with a child with a constellation of extreme traits, you will want to learn how to create a fit that optimizes the child's ability to feel more at peace with himself and with the world. Essentially, goodness of fit is the result of the adults' abilities to recognize the child's traits and surround him with an environment that supports and encourages his natural way of behaving, as much as possible. As the child grows, adults use techniques that soften the edges of the more extreme traits. They help him cope more comfortably, and their management techniques serve to desensitize him and expand his horizons.

Extreme traits, more difficult to manage

In the past, parents were often blamed for a child's behavior problems as if they were solely responsible. Now, we know that many behaviors stem from temperament traits. Caring for a child with an assortment of extreme temperament traits is exhausting and can lead to anger, embarrassment, depression, or guilt in the adult. It can seem like the child is always on center stage, with other people waiting in the wings as supporting actors. Sometimes, adults get locked into very negative patterns of behavior with these children, and the traits become more pronounced, with the child becoming even more fearful, assertive, or clingy.

Take heart! Not only can these behaviors be well managed, it is gratifying to know that, ultimately, these traits can serve the child in a very positive sense. For example, those who are highly sensitive may later use their sensory awareness in artistic ways, such as becoming performers, chefs, or designers. If highly active people can focus their energy and drive, they can thrive in competition. Serious mood people may be drawn to law, journalism, or poetry. And persistent people may find themselves tackling stubborn environmental problems or pursuing scholarly research. Intense people often become charismatic leaders or performers. Each of these traits, when well directed, can manifest itself in positive outcomes.

How to Help the Child

High activity level

- Arrange frequent outdoor play and physically active indoor play, such as dancing, tumbling, jumping on a crib mattress on the floor, etc.

- Make sure young children are not being asked to sit still longer than they can legitimately manage. Change the pace of the day to balance vigorous and calm times. Build in a significant amount of time for physical activity.

- In a group setting, make sure that the traffic patterns of the room allow children to move around without knocking into one another. Section off parts of the room to offer protected areas for quiet play.

High level of regularity

- Stick to a schedule as much as possible, avoiding hunger and naptime issues.

- Bring the child's nighttime lovey, or use a duplicate, when the child needs to sleep away from home.

Withdrawal from new stimuli

- When starting a new play group or child care program, talk about it ahead of time with your child, describing the room or yard and the kinds of activities that will take place there. Try to visit the site ahead of time with your child, to let him or her get a feel for the space.

- Don't pressure the child to politely greet others. Ignore any negative reaction he may have; continue your conversation and allow him to emerge on his own timing.

- Make any challenge manageable by breaking it into smaller steps. Offer praise for trying new activities.

Low adaptability to change

- Whenever possible, plan your day so that you are not rushing the child. Allow extra time for everything.

- Allow your child to explore things and places visually first.

- Prepare your child for new experiences in advance. Explain the sequence of events to your child ahead of time, even for daily activities such as bath or clean-up time.

- Establish a daily routine and stick to it.

High sensory awareness

- Make adjustments to the environment to reduce the harshness of light, color, noise, movement, and smell levels. Put yourself in your child's place: try to imagine how he or she feels spending all day in that space. Reduce any unnecessary sensory bombardment. Create white space on the walls by simplifying displays. Turn down loud music.

- Be strategic about introducing new foods; combine them with existing favorites.

- Avoid overstimulation before naptime or bedtime.

- Help the child label her feelings so she can learn to talk about them rather than go to pieces. Say things like:

  ▶ "I know you feel sensitive to tags. Let's take the tag off with my scissors."

  ▶ "Looks like the noise hurts your ears. Let's cover them up with these muffs."

  ▶ "I can tell that you feel too warm in that coat. Want to take it off now?"

  ▶ "That sun is so bright it is hard to look out the window. Let's put on your sunglasses."

Jackson, a highly sensitive 22-month-old, had started biting children daily at his new child care center. His ten-hour days were spent with twenty-three other toddlers in an overstimulating environment that resembled a circus; it was a constant assault on his senses. Every square inch of wall space was covered in colorful murals, commercially made posters, and bright primary colors. Children's art projects were pinned up helter-skelter everywhere. Mobiles hung low from the ceilings, creating constant movement. Children's music cds blared from the stereo. There was no carpeting or softness available anywhere, just the high shine of vinyl flooring and the hard surfaces of washable furniture. Naptime was the only respite for unhappy Jackson.

Intensity of responses

- Remember that a mild reaction does not mean that a child doesn't have a strong feeling about an experience. Don't discount feelings based on physical reaction. Conversely, don't assume that a child is more upset because he has a loud style of expression.

- When a child erupts, try to stay neutral and calm. Don't get caught up in the moment.

Acknowledge feelings and maintain consistent limits.

■ Use whispering to calm a child; it encourages him to listen to you.

Serious mood or disposition

■ Don't jump to the conclusion that the child is unhappy because he looks serious. Your child's face may register a solemn mood even when he just feels neutral.

■ Point out positive things. Ask, "What was something good that happened today?"

High distractibility

■ Use starter phrases when giving directions or setting limits. It will give the child a chance to ready himself for the coming suggestion. "Justin, *I have an idea for you. Listen. . . .* Let's take the ball outside so it doesn't accidentally knock down your sister's castle," or *"Here's a question for you. . . .* Since it's almost lunchtime, where do you want to sit to eat your lunch? At the kitchen table or on a picnic blanket on the floor?"

■ Consider feeding your child ahead of time if he is too distracted at family mealtimes.

■ Use *anchoring* when disciplining. Rest your hand on the child's arm or shoulder and look him directly in the eye to maintain attention.

■ Turn off or mute the stereo or television or computer when trying to get your child to pay attention to you. Put away the cell phone or other distraction so you can focus on helping your child to focus.

Persistence in activity/attention span

■ Use forewarning when planning to change activities. This gives the child a chance to prepare himself mentally for the change.

■ Schedule plenty of time for your child's favorite activities.

■ Encourage your child to stick with an activity by playing with her, acting as a good role model in trying new ways to use items.

Temperament Worksheet

Creating a Better Fit Between the Child's Temperament and the Environment

Make a copy of this worksheet to jot down various ideas that you have collected from this chapter. As you circle high, moderate, or low for each trait on the left column of the worksheet, refer to the rating scale on pages 51–54 of this chapter. The right column is for your solution ideas.

Name of child: _____ Age: _____ Today's date:_____

Trait	Changes to Make
Activity Level (Circle one: H, M, L) *Notes:*	
Regularity (Circle one: H, M, L) *Notes:*	
Withdrawal/Approach (Circle one: W or A) *Notes:*	

Temperament Worksheet (continued)	
Trait	**Changes to Make**
Adaptability (Circle one: H, M, L) *Notes:*	
Sensory Awareness (Circle one: H, M, L) *Notes:*	
Intensity of Response (Circle one: H, M, L) *Notes:*	
General Mood (Circle one: Positive or Negative) *Notes:*	

Temperament Worksheet (continued)	
Trait	**Changes to Make**
Distractibility (Circle one: H, M, L) *Notes:*	
Persistence in Activity (Circle one: H, M, L) *Notes:*	

Action Review 5

Question 5: *What role does the child's temperament play in the behavior?*

Put a check in the boxes of any actions that you think might help the biting child. In Part IV, you will refer to this list as you fill out an Action Plan worksheet.

❑ Be mindful of how much time the child needs to physically move around during the day.

Notes: _____

_____

❑ For children with high regularity, minimize changes to the daily schedule.

Notes: _____

_____

❏ Give the child enough time to ease into new situations without pressure.

Notes: _____

_____

❏ Take time to forewarn the child about new experiences. Don't rush.

Notes: _____

_____

❏ Make any necessary adjustments to the environment to avoid overstimulation.

Notes: _____

_____

❏ Give the child labels for feelings and give him or her the chance to express them.

Notes: _____

_____

❏ Stay calm during the child's intense expression of emotion.

Notes: _____

_____

❏ Point out the positives when you have an opportunity.

Notes: _____

_____

❏ Use starter phrases and anchoring to get the child's attention.

Notes: _____

_____

❏ Give plenty of advance notice about a change in routine or an end to the activity.

Notes: _____

_____

❏ What else might you want to consider to help this child?

Notes: _____

_____

Question 6

What Effect Does the Physical Environment of the Home or Early Childhood Program Have on the Child?

Environment is a key component in shaping human behavior and often a contributing factor in a child's hurtful behavior. As young children explore the world around them, they use the environment in increasingly sophisticated ways to build on their knowledge of themselves and the larger world. Their environments should be steeped in sensory experiences that are positive, educational, and enriching, not stressful and frustrating. Providing the optimum environment for young children is a heavy responsibility since children have no choice but to be in the environments we create for them, whether at home or at an early childhood program.

Sometimes, a tour of the child's environment (home-based care or center-based care) will reveal issues with the design of the indoor and outdoor spaces. Some spaces are crowded, bright, noisy, and overstimulating, while others may be dull, bland, and lack suitable toys and equipment. Environments like these may be stressful for children and can induce problem behavior. An especially aggressive child in the group may serve as a barometer for the rest of the group, acting out some of the stress that others are feeling. Meaningful changes may range from purchasing new toys, equipment, or furniture to simply rearranging the space and items in the space, or changing its scheduled use. Improvements like these can benefit all of the users of the space. This chapter will help you identify potential problem areas both at home and at the early childhood program, ones that you will consider in drawing up your Action Plan.

Crowded conditions

Nothing creates feelings of tension and stress faster than having to endure crowded conditions. Even many adults become cranky and tense while crammed into a crowded space. But most adults have well-developed impulse control and realize that, whether on a subway, in a shopping center, or on a crowded airplane, the length of time those conditions must be endured is limited. Young children don't possess the same skills for keeping themselves calm when cramped or crowded. They may act out in a show of frustrated aggression under those circumstances. Hurtful behavior often happens when young children are sitting together at lunchtime, circle time, playing in the block corner, or in the sandbox. For children, being too close can feel threatening and overwhelming. Ideally, the amount of space available should allow them to feel calm and secure.

Inadequate play spaces

In many programs, the number of children on the playground exceeds the actual number of play spaces or activities available for them. Think of this like musical chairs: when the music stops, the person without a chair is not going to be happy. Young children have short attention spans, and they need a well-stocked assortment of daily activities to choose from in order to avoid quarreling over shortages. Studies show that a lack of play spaces has been a predictor of problem behavior. Caregivers and parents must be vigilant in providing enough activities, equipment, and props for children. Sometimes, favorite equipment wears out and does not get readily replaced, resulting in frequent fights over the last remaining item.

How to assess the number of play spaces

When counting the play spaces available in a child's group environment, look for one and one-half to two play spaces per child. For example, in a group of twelve toddlers there should be eighteen to twenty-four play spaces outside as well as inside. You can count up the play spaces in any situation by asking yourself:

- How many children can comfortably use the housekeeping area together?
- How many children can utilize the climber at one time without congestion?
- How many riding toys are in working order?
- How many children can comfortably play in this block corner at any one time?
- How many balls are out today?
- How many children can spread out and use the puzzle table at once?

Lack of novelty

In settings where children must interact with the same old toys in the same old ways, boredom can easily set in, leading to hurtful behavior. Young children learn what they need to know from a toy fairly quickly. In an environment that is optimally responsive to their needs, adults will pick up on cues that children are ready for something new and will vary the environment to maintain high levels of novelty.

Lack of loose parts

One easy way to inject novelty is to make sure an environment contains enough "loose parts." Loose parts are the props of playtime: toys that don't have a right or wrong function and can be used in a multitude of creative ways. These open-ended activities are developmentally appropriate at many levels from toddler to school-age, leading to sharing, turn-taking, and other positive social interactions. Siblings can successfully play together or sit near each other when offered loose parts at home. Children of all ages use these kinds of materials in ways that are inherently satisfying and creative since there is no right or wrong way. Sitting near a sibling and playing with the same materials, but each in their own way, gives children a chance to enjoy each other's company, chat about what they are doing, and strengthen fragile emotional bonds. Both early childhood programs and home settings can become rich in loose parts with some thoughtful shopping.

Examples of loose parts:
Sand and water play toys
Wheel toys of various sizes
Balls
Blocks and other building-type manipulative toys
Housekeeping pretend play items
Art supplies: paint, glue, collage materials, sidewalk chalk, craft materials and recycled items
Dolls, stuffed animals, action figures
Doll house with figures
Dress-up clothes
Play dough and dough tools

Lack of materials, indoors and outdoors

A property dispute is the number one reported reason for biting and fighting. An easy fix is to assess the play materials found in the child's environment and add what is lacking to it, at home or elsewhere. As was discussed in the first chapter, toddlers and twos are developmentally still fairly egocentric. They are just learning how to curb their impulses, share, take turns, and be patient, but they are not accomplished at these skills. Especially in toddler programs, it can be wise to invest in duplicates of *favorite* items to avoid endless tussling.

Lack of age-appropriate items

Sometimes parents spend money on the purchase of nice new toys and equipment that only briefly hold a child's interest. The toys may still seem brand new to adults, but remember that children are developing at lightning speed. They learn what they need from items and are ready to move on to the next challenge. Parents and caregivers reduce boredom and stretch the value of toys by strategically selecting materials. As explained earlier, loose parts and open-ended materials can be used creatively in many different ways by different age groups. Also, make sure to have challenging skill-building materials for toddlers and twos. They are ready for more complexity, such as shape sorting, puzzles, matching games, etc.

Mixed-age challenges

Offering age-appropriate toys can be especially difficult for parents who have more than one child and for caregivers who operate family child care homes. The adults may be caring for infants, toddlers, preschoolers, and even school-agers all under the same roof and in the same rooms. It can be tricky to find space for children to play with items that are challenging for them, while keeping choking hazards away from infants and toddlers. In this situation, adults need to get very creative in ways to schedule the day and break up the home spaces. Find ways to give older children enough time and room for using their complex materials while still protecting the infants and younger children. Make sure all children get a chance to stretch their cognitive skills.

Lack of soft elements

Toddler-savvy adults surround toddlers with washable surfaces whenever possible, since toddlers frequently get into messy activities. Sometimes, children's whole worlds are filled with hard edges, washable surfaces, and vinyl and plastic. Observations of young children in group settings have revealed that antisocial behaviors can sometimes be softened or positively impacted by introducing elements of softness into their world. When children have places to go to refuel and calm themselves, they are better able to re-enter a larger group in ways that are socially positive. High quality child development programs make sure that they have soft alcoves, cozy corners, or semi-private spaces in which children can find that kind of relief for themselves. Many elements can be added to a room to provide softness and induce calmer behavior:

Items that create softness:

Carpeting	Hanging houseplants
Adult laps	Couches and soft chairs
Stuffed animals	Hanging mobiles and kites
Soft lighting	Pillows and blankets
Fabric curtains	Quilts hanging on walls
Fabric samples	Soft music
Pets	Canopies

Too much stimulation versus too little

Environments contain sensory stimuli that affect how people feel and react to each other. All people experience their environment through touch, sound, sight, smell, and taste. In the preceding section, we have already discussed touch and the importance of softness in the environment. But other senses, particularly hearing and seeing, are also crucial and play a big part in how children interpret and react to their environment. A child whose body is overloaded with sensory information experiences a physiological response that generates emotional reactions. High-load settings (such as subways or shopping centers) act as stressors, increasing feelings of fun and excitement or causing feelings of discomfort and frantic, anxious behaviors. Low-load settings (such as bedrooms or libraries) provide a more calming or even dulling influence.

Visual stimulation

Color is a critical component of any environment. A good deal of research has been done on how color affects people. Red actually raises the blood pres-

> Liam, 17 months old, spent six hours a day in a well-stocked, nicely furnished infant/toddler room. There were plenty of developmentally appropriate toys, soft elements, calming colors, and even a large fish tank set low to the floor. A play yard was right outside the door, complete with sand, shade, low climbing structure, toddler riding toys, etc. Unfortunately, Liam had been biting every day for weeks, even though provided with close supervision. With more than a dozen biting attempts per day, caregivers began putting him in a playpen after each bite, while attending to the bitten child. Interestingly, Liam loved being in the playpen and protested when taken out. He seemed relieved somehow to be put into that smaller, protected space. Liam was a highly sensitive child. He felt overwhelmed by the overall dynamics of the group size: twenty-four children and six adults. Eventually, his parents moved him to a family child care home with only six children, and the biting immediately stopped.

sure, increases respiration, and promotes use of large motor functions. Blue has a more calming effect on the heart rate and respiratory system. Green is the most restful color to the eye, while violet supports contemplative and peaceful activities.

Visual stimulation can either be aesthetically pleasing and engaging, or it can over-whelm children and create feelings of scattered focus. Over-decorated settings, where every square inch of wall space is covered, sometimes in a glaring and garish manner, can result in a headache-inducing cacophony of images. Children's clothing and toys of bright primary colors provide another level of visual stimulation. People behave differently in different set-tings, taking cues from their surroundings. People with a high sensory awareness, who feel even minimal effects strongly, may act out negatively as a reaction to intense stimuli. When the amount of stimuli is modified, their behavior becomes modified, too.

Noise
Noise has a strong effect on people for whom high noise levels can even be painful. Many early childhood programs and homes are very noisy. These settings may include a constantly blaring television, the loud conversations of family members, and/or background music that never stops. When noise is constant, distracting, and pervasive, it can be harder for children to concentrate on tasks or make good choices about their actions. It can lead to over-excitability, or it can drive children to look for places to withdraw and retreat. Both are extremes of emotional expression.

Smells
Strong smells can have a big impact on people who have an enhanced sense of smell or are super-sensitive to fragrances. Some children react vehemently to cleaning product odors. Others are highly affected by body odor, cigarette smoke, mold, sunscreen, lotions, perfumes, soap, air fresheners, and flowers. Sometimes these people get nauseous, have headaches, and become emotionally upset. Listen for ongoing complaints from children about smells so that you can try to reduce any unnecessary sensory assault.

Reasonable expectations
Sometimes biting behavior happens when structured group times last too long. Toddlers and two-year-olds have short attention spans. If caregivers are spending too much time trying to corral the group to keep their attention, it may be that the organized group time is simply longer than appropriate or not physically active enough.

Proactive and supportive adults
While it is true that young children learn through exploring their world individually and playing together side-by-side, a child can definitely benefit by having adults nearby to comment on what he is doing, lending support during social-emotional interactions. Especially when hurtful behavior happens during unstructured, free play times, children who bite may be helped by proactive adult interactions. By commenting on what is happening and offering new ideas for how to use the materials, adults are injecting structure into the play. Though subtle, this informed structure helps to keep children engaged, extends their play, and helps them find new ways to explore their environment in pro-social ways.

Patterns and themes of biting episodes

When looking for root causes of why a child may be acting out, match the biting incidents with the daily schedule to see if any themes emerge. For example, a child may succumb to aggression because most of the activity areas have been *closed,* creating aimless wandering and boredom. You may also find that a child is biting others just before lunchtime when supervision is less, while one of the teachers has gone inside to put mats down for naptime. Maybe the child is biting while waiting for a perennially late snack time; he just doesn't have the mental energy to control his impulses any longer. Perhaps the behavior happens at the end of the day when supervision is less focused because teachers are busy talking to incoming parents.

How to Help the Child

Reduce cramped conditions

- Break up a large group into smaller groups whenever possible.

- Seat children in ways that provide sufficient personal space at their tables.

- Reassess the room arrangement and make changes as needed to assure better flow and less congestion. Read *Caring Spaces, Learning Places* by Jim Greenman for more information.

- In group care, caregivers should not bunch up, sitting together during free play time, but rather spread out, which encourages the children to use the entire room.

- Remove unnecessary furniture to allow more room for floor play.

- If possible, add a play loft to increase the amount of play space available.

- Sit between children when reading stories, etc.

- Bathe children separately if dealing with bath time behavior problems.

- Make sure children have enough play space indoors and out. Consider making temporary changes to shared spaces by moving the coffee table aside to make room for more floor play, etc.

- Combat small space syndrome by taking children outside to expel energy as often as possible, or jump around and dance inside to lively music.

Have enough play materials and numbers of play spaces

- Evaluate the toys and materials available to children. Are they mostly outgrown baby toys? Update your toy selection regularly.

- Do specific items create frustration for children? Would some step-by-step help prove useful? Set aside time to guide the child through use of the items.

- Are you providing *open-ended toys,* such as loose parts, toys that can be used in a wide variety of ways and in interesting combinations? Or are they mostly *close-ended toys,* with a clear cut purpose, such as a puzzle or a shape-sorting ball? If so, the child may lose interest more quickly. Provide an assortment of both open-ended and close-ended materials.

- Are the adults involved saying "No" often? If so, why are there so many restrictions? If items need to be put out of reach, create storage for them so you have less worry about damage or safety.

- Create safe places for young children to use their toys away from crawling infants. Use low portable fences to cordon off sections of a house or playroom. Set up a play space at a table or a counter, where the child can play without having to fend off a curious infant.

- Find a mother's helper, a young teenager or preteen, who can occasionally come over to play with your child while you are still at home to supervise, as you take care of other activities.

- Assess the number of play spaces in your home and yard that are available to the children during various times of day. Add activities if necessary.

Control the amount of stimulation

- Attempt to listen to and look at the setting from the child's point of view, not your own.

- Use music strategically to influence behavior in positive ways. Play soothing music when children are distraught or tense.

- Be aware of how noise levels may be revving up the child, especially in confined spaces, and make changes as necessary.

- Be more purposeful in your television viewing and radio listening. Limit the background noise.

- Be aware of how ultra-rich visual settings, such as the grocery store, can overly stimulate and influence a child's behavior. Limit the time your child spends in these settings if you think it is contributing to behavior difficulties.

Action Review 6

Question 6: *What effect does the physical environment of the home or early childhood program have on the child?*

Put a check in the boxes of any actions that you think might help the biting child. In Part IV, you will refer to this list as you fill out an Action Plan worksheet.

❑ Reduce cramped conditions.

Notes: _____

_____

❏ Create sufficient play spaces with an adequate number of toys.

Notes: _____

_____

❏ Provide novelty with use of loose parts.

Notes: _____

_____

❏ Provide age-appropriate toys and materials.

Notes: _____

_____

❏ Add softness to the environment.

Notes: _____

_____

❏ Reduce sensory overstimulation.

Notes: _____

_____

❏ Increase sensory understimulation.

Notes: _____

_____

❏ Adjust daily schedule.

Notes: _____

_____

❏ Interact with the child during free play.

Notes: _____

_____

❏ Set reasonable expectations for waiting times.

Notes: _____

_____

❏ What else might you want to consider to help this child?

Notes: _____

_____

Question 7

What Kind of Limit Setting Is the Child Experiencing at Home and with Other Caregivers or Teachers?

While developing the Action Plan it is crucial to understand the child's past and current experiences with *limit setting,* also commonly referred to as *discipline.* Having a clear understanding of the type of discipline being used by the adults in the child's life will enable you to focus on whether you need to either augment or alter the interactions. It may be that the child is confused by conflicting rules, broad expectations, negative handling, or inconsistent management.

Boundaries: Setting Limits for Young Children

Young children have much to learn about their world; however, they are at a distinct disadvantage because they don't know their boundaries yet. At this tender age, young children's actions can put them in harm's way, so adults set limits or boundaries to protect them from danger and allow them to test their wings in small ways.

Establishing these boundaries for young children can be compared to setting the fence posts of a corral, the kind of fencing used for a baby horse to provide safety and security. Caregivers and parents define the actual boundaries of this fence as they decide where to draw the line, where to set limits on a child's behavior ("I won't let you grab that from David."). They look for ways to give the child some control and freedom over her actions within the safe confines of the boundaries. They let the child make some choices while still maintaining overall control over daily needs. ("Shall we change your diaper in the bedroom or in the bathroom?" or "Do you want to have your bath now or after dinner?")

As a child grows she learns to manage herself within the limits you set (exhibiting self-discipline). You are gradually able to extend the limits or fence to allow even more freedom and self-control. ("Are you ready for lunch now or do you want to play outside a while longer?" or "Which coat do you think you will need today?") Parents continue to expand the limits to give her more sophisticated choices, privileges, and rewards, where she can make more of her own choices and experience the consequences. ("If you can complete your homework before Saturday night, you may have Cindy come to our house for a sleepover.") As a child matures she needs fewer and fewer limits because she has internalized self-discipline and has learned smart decision-making skills.

Pushing on boundaries, testing the limits

Typically, a child of any age will test the boundaries that have been set for her, to see if the adult will yield and under what condition. She needs to see how much power she has over these boundaries. If she didn't push up against the boundary or limit, she wouldn't learn how firm it is! Young children push against boundaries by throwing tantrums, hitting, biting, grabbing, running away, and resisting bath time, meal time, bedtime, etc. It's perfectly normal for children to push on boundaries at every stage of their development to test the limits of their power and to understand their role in the world in relation to others.

Self-control is the goal

The ultimate goal of limit setting is to teach children self-control, helping children learn what *to do* (instead of simply what to avoid doing). Children's difficult feelings are acknowledged during discipline, while the limits are consistently maintained for safety and cooperation. Adults using this method teach children about alternative choices to misbehavior and reward them for making the right choices. Children who are well managed through positive discipline techniques develop better self-control and better decision-making capabilities, and are better at handling their own anger. These children start life with more concrete experiences in learning to share and cooperate, skills that come in handy as they expand their social horizons beyond the family.

Understanding the perspective of others

Learning to recognize and understand the thoughts, feelings, and intentions of others makes it easier for a child to manage her own difficult feelings. Along the way she learns to inhibit the impulse to strike out instantly. She is better able to interpret what is going on in a situation by sizing it up and looking at it from another's point of view. Researchers call this having good "perspective-taking" skills. Children who can assess a situation in this way are more successful in dealing with people in general. Parents and teachers can help teach these skills by the way they talk about other people's intentions and thoughts.

Styles of reacting to a child's boundary-testing behavior

Authoritarian: Command and control

Some people *overreact* to boundary testing. They smash the child down when restating the limit, using ultra-strong punishments when children misbehave. They see each incident of testing as a personal challenge to their authority and respond in an authoritarian command-and-control style, demanding that their orders be observed.

> When Julio bumped into Ariel while standing in line, she shot him a look of surprise and said, "Hey, be careful!" Rather than assume he had meant to harm her (and immediately pushing him back), she had quickly sized up the situation and realized that it was probably just an accident.

Permissive: Wishy-washy and vague

Some people *underreact* to boundary testing. They let the child widen or push the boundary aside prematurely, loosening limits at the emotional insistence of their child. They have an aversion to conflict and are willing to live by their child's whims, with very little discipline in place.

Authoritative: Firm and warm

The healthiest approach is known as *authoritative*. With this style, adults don't scare children into minding them, nor do they acquiesce to them. Rather, they *stay firm and warm* and use discipline based on their knowledge of child development and each child's specific capabilities. When a child tests a limit, the adult reiterates the limit and follows through using a matter-of-fact firm demeanor and logical consequences. This style allows for children's natural inclination to test the boundaries placed around them. If they see that the limit stands in spite of their own fussing and fuming, they gain comfort from that.

Children more easily accept boundaries that are clear; they often rebel against boundaries that are vague. Once children become convinced, through their own testing, that a particular limit isn't going anywhere, they move on to testing others. As they discover where all of the boundaries are, they stop testing them and spend more time on activities within the boundaries that are fun and comforting or challenging and stimulating. (For a comprehensive discussion of effective authoritative parenting and limit setting for children ages two through twelve, read Elizabeth Crary's clear, practical *STAR Parenting Tales and Tools*.)

What to Avoid When Responding to Biting

Shame and guilt

Some people try to explain to children that they should change their negative behavior for the express purpose of being nice to others. They say things like "Don't bite people, it's not nice," or "How do you think that feels?" or "How would you like it if she bit you?" or "See how you made her cry? Shame on you! How could you do that to your friend?" Using shame and guilt to admonish a child for not being nice makes no sense; "being nice" was never her intention in the first place! The child bit someone because of her own egocentric view of the world. She was experiencing some kind of confusion, tension, sensitivity, or pressure. Maybe she was feeling bored, crowded, threatened, hungry, or tired. Maybe she was exhibiting emotional behavior she had seen elsewhere, or she was copying the way someone treated her earlier. Telling a child she shouldn't bite "because it isn't nice" is simply a waste of breath.

Forcing an apology

Asking a toddler or two-year-old to apologize after biting is standard operating procedure in many homes and early childhood programs. The goal is to encourage the child to be accountable, penitent, and humbled by her misdeed. It also is meant to give the victim the satisfaction of some sort of closure. While these intentions are worthy, in reality, that is not the end result. Typically, the child can learn to repeat those words but it doesn't mean she actually feels any remorse. More often than not, she learns that saying "I'm sorry" is just an easy way to get out of trouble. It is not unusual for these children to then bite someone else later in the day, quickly saying "I'm sorry, I'm sorry" afterward. The adults involved are often completely flummoxed. They had hoped that the incident had been settled after the utterance of an apology, lesson learned. Unfortunately, the child learned only to parrot the words, not alter her behavior. Be assured that, as children grow, they are more able to feel empathy, express remorse, and respond appropriately. Model compassion, and eventually the child will express it authentically.

Self-fulfilling prophecy: Being overheard by your child

Dealing with toddlers and young children is an exhausting undertaking. Adults often need to share their trials and tribulations with friends and colleagues. Sometimes, however, they do it within earshot of the child. Listening to how others talk about him fuels the image he is developing of himself. When a child hears himself defined in a certain way, it can become a self-fulfilling prophecy. Parents may say, "I don't know what to do anymore. Trevor bites somebody at child care almost every day. He's like a little wild animal. Everyone is afraid of him." Highlighting a child's challenging behaviors within earshot of the child unknowingly contributes to the problem because it brands the child with negative traits.

| Ten Things to Avoid When Responding to Biting ||
Action	Why is that action a problem?
Expecting behavior that is too mature	Child is blamed unfairly for not measuring up
Not expecting age-appropriate behavior	Child is not held accountable for things she can easily manage to learn and do
Using fear, threats, or force	Creates distrust; gives child no helpful information or alternative behaviors to use
Allowing the hurtful child to tend to the victim	Puts the hurtful child on center stage
Shouting, ranting at the child	Child either feels powerful for instigating such a strong reaction OR feels scared by it
Using time-out with children under 2½ years	Not seen as a deterrent by a toddler
Spanking or hitting a child	Child learns it is okay to for a stronger person to hit a weaker person. Causes resentment and provides no constructive advice or skills
Sarcasm, teasing, or name calling	Mean-spirited, causes mistrust and resentment. Names have a way of sticking, branding a child negatively and harming self-esteem
Biting child back to show him "how it feels"	Breeds fear, distrust, and resentment
Forcing a bitter taste into child's mouth	Child feels shock and rage at being accosted

During circle time, a teacher introduced the children to the concept of rhythm by gently slapping her hands on her knees twice and clapping her hands together once, saying, "One, two, three . . . one, two, three . . ." The group copied her actions over and over. Afterward, several children clamored to show her how they could do this rhythm game on their own. "Well done, you got the rhythm," she said to each one, as the children beamed with pride.

Meaningless praise

Praise and encouragement are valuable commodities to a young child. Sometimes parents go "over-the-top" in lavishing praise on young children for every little thing, thus diluting its effectiveness and integrity. After a while, overly enthusiastic praise becomes meaningless. If you find yourself sounding forced and searching for new ways to praise your child, you are probably using too much praise. There are five main types of praise: descriptive, appreciative, reflective (three helpful types), evaluative, and exaggerated (two harmful types).

Effective praise

- **Descriptive** praise gives a picture of what you liked, similar to the way a sportscaster talks about action on the field. "I see you and your brother are sharing the blocks and building a beautiful castle."

- **Appreciative** praise is a personal expression from an adult regarding the child's efforts. It is especially meaningful to a child when she automatically complies with a limit or when she does something without being asked. "I like the way you held my hand in the parking lot. Well done, Maia."

- **Reflective** praise describes behavior you liked and asks the child a question, such as "You just gave Antonio a turn with the scooter he had been waiting for. How did that make you feel?"

Ineffective praise

- **Evaluative** praise judges a person's actions or achievements. If used in a vague, clipped way, it can confuse a child as to exactly why he or she deserved the praise. The overall value of the praise is diluted when the same phrase is used over and over again for every little thing. Also, the behavior is less likely to be repeated because the child's actions were not identified, as in "Good job," or "Good girl."

- **Exaggerated** praise goes overboard on rating a child. It often focuses on your assessment of the child's character, rather than on the child's own effort or strategy. This kind of praise skews the child's view of herself, reduces an adult's credibility, and paints an unrealistic picture of a child's character, contribution, or accomplishments. Children growing up in homes that lavish this type of overly dramatic praise can feel that doing anything less than perfectly will make them a big disappointment to parents. When parents set the bar so high, children sometimes stop trying new things. The fear of failing is too strong. Examples: "That magnificent easel painting should be hanging in an art gallery somewhere!" "You are the prettiest girl in the world!" "You are the fastest runner I know!" "That's the biggest tower I've ever seen!" "You're an absolute genius!"

How to Help the Child

Keep discipline simple

- Distill limit setting to one main message. For example, all of your techniques will lead to the following concept: "Even when we feel upset, we show it without hurting other people, ourselves, or things." ("Hurt" refers to both physical and emotional hurt.) Be as succinct as possible whenever you need to restate the house or school rules or when emphasizing directions. For young toddlers that can mean using one word directions, such as "stop," "come," "sit." Older toddlers can handle two-word directions more easily, "touch gently" or "hold hands." As children get older continue to be as clear as possible, still using only a handful of words to sum up the rule you want to emphasize. Examples: "Coats belong in the closet." "Lunch boxes are kept in cubbies." "Food is for eating." "Inside stores, people walk; at the park you may run." "When puzzles get put together, they go back on the shelf."

Insert yourself strategically

- Keep a close eye on young children at play and be ready to step in to shift a child's attention away from a potential problem. Become skilled at looking at the world through the eyes of a child to see which moments cause distress. You may be able to gently insert yourself ahead of time as a good model of pro-social play. Example: "Look over there . . . I see another sand cup for your cooking play. Now you both have one," or "Come with me to find the water brushes in the shed. The sidewalk needs to be painted today. Let's get two brushes and find a friend to join us."

Stay calm during tantrums

- During a temper tantrum, don't give in to a child's demands out of your own embarrassment or fatigue. Stay calm and say, "I can see how mad you are right now. When you are all done crying, we can talk about it." Don't try to talk her out of her tantrum. Just go about your business, keeping an eye on her from a bit of a distance. Calmly labeling her feelings reduces her need to act them out since you have recognized and acknowledged them. This should help her to pull herself together more quickly, at which point you can discuss the situation calmly.

  It may help to think of yourself as an actor, pretending that the tantrums don't bother you, because it will likely be hard to wait them out. Rest assured that your calm response will project the message that your child is entitled to be upset but it won't have the effect of swaying your decision. If your child is throwing a tantrum in a place that is unsafe, like at your feet in the kitchen, calmly pick the child up and move him or her to a safer location. Example: "Ethan, I'm moving you to the hallway. This is a better place for crying—there is more room here. As soon as you are all done crying and ready to talk, come on over so we can figure things out." You want to project a nonjudgmental attitude and acceptance, while demonstrating that even a powerful outburst like a temper tantrum does not crumble you or your limit.

Be attentive

■ Provide plenty of opportunities for authentic positive attention. When playing with the child, don't do three other things simultaneously. This dilutes the quality of your time together and gives children mixed messages about your interest in them. Research has shown that fifteen to twenty minutes of quality time with a parent dramatically reduces acting-out behavior in children. To have the most impact, this one-on-one activity between parent and child should be daily, predictable, and spent in child-directed play. Multitasking by sitting near your child and watching the news while she plays on the floor with blocks doesn't count as quality time from the child's point of view. You must authentically interact with your child and talk about what she is doing and thinking during play. Example: "What a sturdy bridge you made! Look, it's tall enough for your boat to go under it. Is there a little car we could use, to drive on top of the bridge? That's really fun! What else shall we build?"

Take a breath and stay focused

■ Take a deep breath and blow it out before stepping into a volatile situation. A few seconds won't delay your response long, but it will give you a moment to gather your senses and make a purposeful instead of frantic statement.

■ When dealing with chronic biting, keep the Biting Solution Pocket Guide (page 121) with all the phrases you want to use handy. Stay focused and consistent. Don't wing it or your emotions will take over. Also, skipping steps during intervention will leave holes in the child's ability to understand and change. Just describe the problem in a simple way while you sort out how to proceed. Resist the urge to get preachy. "Stop, Matt. Right now! I can see you want this trike but I won't let you bite people. We'll talk about this in a few minutes." Before you can talk with the biter any further, you will be busy with the victim.

Alternatives to an apology

■ Model apologetic behavior by describing what you feel in the presence of both the biting child and the bitten child. Say, "Mary, I am so sorry about what happened to your finger. You must be in a lot of pain right now. Come sit on my lap until you feel better."

■ Rather than force an apology, ask the biting child to let the other child know that he is "All done _____ [biting, hitting, kicking, etc.]." This is more believable and authentic than a forced apology. Say, "Jason, Meredith is worried that you are going to bite her again. If you are all done biting now, please tell her that with your words."

Teach compassion

- Help the child understand that her behavior is not acceptable while demonstrating that you recognize her feelings. "I know that you were upset and angry that Niklas took the ball, but I can't let you hurt him."

- Look for every opportunity to teach compassion. Utilize books, puppets, dolls, television shows, and your own experiences. Label what you see and what you feel. Don't stick to words like happy, sad, and mad. Look for interesting words that describe nuanced feelings, such as frustrated, bothered, nervous, worried, relieved, scared, and embarrassed.

- Offer a way for one child to help another manage waiting for a turn with a coveted item. To the child using the hammer, say, "Liam, can you see how Derrick is watching you? He is waiting patiently to try out the hammer when you are done. I wonder . . . how many more minutes do you need with it? Eight minutes . . . or ten minutes?" Liam gets the power to pick a number (or perhaps offer another number), and the child who is waiting gets the benefit of knowing there is a finite amount of time he or she must wait. Setting a timer works well for siblings, as well as groups of young children, adding an element of productive action to the waiting. Even two-year-olds can use this tool, saying, "When you done?" as they rein in the impulse to strike out under stress.

Teach perspective-taking skills

- Help children learn to interpret another child's intentions by posing questions while reading stories: "Why did the boy feel sad?" "What do you think he will do next?"

- Comment on what you see so they can hear how you appraise a situation: "I'm noticing that Gina is having a hard time sharing this book. I think she needs a chance to use this book all by herself in the cozy corner."

Offer meaningful praise

- Don't overwhelm a child with exaggerated or meaningless praise. It reduces your credibility. For toddlers, keep your praise simple and specific.

- Comment on the action accomplished, not the child: "Thank you for putting the cups away for me." "You asked Jenny for a turn. Good job." "That was helpful—you made room for Roberto to sit down next to you."

- Reward with praise small moments of self-regulation: "I know it's hard to wait. You are being so patient. Well done."

- Deliver your praise or encouragement in your natural voice. Save celebration-style expressions for very special accomplishments or efforts where over-the-top recognition is appropriate.

- Help the child learn to appreciate social accomplishments: "You must feel proud of sharing your markers with Justin. He looks happy to have such a good friend."

- Sometimes nonverbal praise will suffice to let a child know you noticed his good behavior: pat on the back, wink of the eye, blown kiss, big smile, silent clapping, high five, or thumbs up.

- Watch for times to compliment the child when you see him use behaviors that communicate stressful feelings in appropriate ways. Examples include:

  ▶ When they use words to confront another child instead of using hurtful behavior ("Please don't do that," "Move away from me," "I don't like that," "Don't," "Mine").

  ▶ When they play peaceably near others in the sandbox or at the table.

  ▶ When he grits his teeth and makes guttural sounds, such as growling like a bear, or stomps his feet instead of biting to express anger or frustration.

Action Review 7

Question 7: *"What kind of limit setting is the child currently experiencing at home and with other caregivers?"*

Put a check in the boxes of any actions that you think might help the biting child. In Part IV, you will refer to this list as you fill out an Action Plan worksheet.

❏ Develop an authoritative limit-setting philosophy.
Notes: _____

_____

❏ Insert yourself to promote pro-social play.
Notes: _____

_____

❏ Stay calm during tantrums.
Notes: _____

_____

❏ Avoid giving negative attention.
Notes: _____

_____

❏ Give authentic positive attention.
Notes: _____

_____

❏ Pause to gather your thoughts before responding.
Notes: _____

_____

❑ Model apologetic behavior; don't force an apology.

Notes: _____

_____

❑ Model compassion and empathy.

Notes: _____

_____

❑ Use meaningful and specific praise, not broad and untrue statements.

Notes: _____

_____

❑ What else might you want to consider to help this child?

Notes: _____

_____

Part III

Case Studies

In Part III, you will see how the Seven Questions can be used to help children who are struggling with different types of biting problems. All of these customized Action Plans were developed from actual cases. While the gender, ages, and situations are the same, the names of the children have all been changed.

Information related to the Seven Questions was gathered through direct observation of the children and interviews with parents and teachers or caregivers. The customized Action Plans that follow are the actual plans developed by and for the families, caregivers, and teachers.

Toddlers
Ethan: Biting Games, Body Boundaries, and High Energy
Sophia: Bad Habits, Challenging Temperament, and Boring Toys

Two-Year-Olds
Lukas: Bottles, Blame, and Boredom
Abigail: Divorce, Negative Attention, and Family Day Care Dynamic

Three-Year-Old
Jayden: Social Inexperience, Speech Problems, and Sibling Issues

Ethan, 18 Months Old

Biting Games, Body Boundaries, and High Energy

Background

Ethan had been in the same large infant-toddler room at a center since the age of three months. He had a playful, positive mood and cheerful personality. Recently, he had started biting, and it had become more frequent, happening every day, several times a day. The center was used to dealing with biting behavior, seeing it as a common occurrence among groups of toddlers. Ethan's biting behavior, however, had turned chronic. Given the fact that the group was a mixture of infants and toddlers, many of the youngest children in the program were especially vulnerable. The caregivers at this center were highly skilled but had trouble keeping up with Ethan's habitual biting. Most of the biting happened on the playground, at snack time, at lunch time, or right after naptime. Complaints from parents poured into the office. While they regretted it, the child care center gave the parents an ultimatum: Ethan had to get this biting under control or he would be expelled.

Ethan lived with his very young mom and dad and their large golden retriever dog. His parents were devastated that their child was causing such a problem, and they were extremely motivated to do anything they could to help stop the biting. They had a large extended family and were getting plenty of support from their relatives. Ethan was the first grandchild; his grandparents enjoyed indulging him at every opportunity. At home, Ethan rarely experienced frustration or disappointment. At the center, of course, his needs were not supreme.

Observation and Interview Results

1. Social/Emotional development

Ethan was very large for his age and well coordinated. In body type, he took after his dad, who was an especially large, athletic man. Ethan had earned the nickname of "Bulldozer" for the way he moved through the room, seemingly unaware that others felt uncomfortable or intimidated by his actions. He did not yet understand how to recognize or respect physical boundaries between himself and others. During play he was constantly pushing up against or leaning into people awkwardly. Ethan had a love of large motor toys and could happily ride around on them for 15 to 20 minutes at a time. He enjoyed being near adults and liked to make them laugh with his antics. All in all, Ethan was the kind of toddler who exemplified the phrase, "the world is his oyster."

2. Past experiences and recent changes

While Ethan had seen other people bitten at child care, he had not ever been bitten himself. On the home front, the main experience he had with rough-and-tumble activities was with his dog Sarge. Since he had been able to crawl, he had chased after, pulled himself up on, and grabbed toys away from the good-natured and long-suffering dog. He and his dad played wrestling games with Sarge all the time on their living room carpet.

And, most significant, for months now both his mom and dad had delighted in playing biting games with Ethan, such as nibbling on his toes or tummy and saying, "You are so yummy, I'm going to eat you right up!"

3. Verbal skills

Ethan had trouble expressing himself verbally, partly due to previous ear infections. He already had a long history of ear infections, more than ten infections before the age of one year, although he now appeared to be hearing adequately. While Ethan could point to body parts and imitate the sounds of various animals, he was not putting words together into two- or three-word sentences yet.

4. Physical condition

Ethan's ear infections were on the decline now, fortunately, so the pain he had been experiencing had subsided. He was teething, of course, but seemed to take that in stride. Physically, Ethan was a healthy, normal toddler. Because Ethan used up so much energy, he was a ravenous eater and an early napper. Ethan generally awoke from his nap about 2:30, but snack was not served until 3:30 when *all* the toddlers were awake. During that hour, Ethan and a handful of other toddlers had to stay in the room and play quietly while waiting for their snack. In looking at the biting trends, it was noted that many of the bites occurred during that hour.

5. Temperament traits

Ethan was impulsive and impatient, showing difficulty with waiting for things. He could be very persistent in his play with certain kinds of activities that captured his attention, such as riding toys and water play. He was very adaptable to new situations, even fearless when faced with an interesting new challenge. He showed his emotions intensely, never leaving adults to wonder how he felt about anything. His parents found him to be a fairly easy-to-raise child, even though his activity level sometimes left them breathless and afraid to take their eyes off of him for a minute.

6. Physical environment

Ethan's child care room had twenty-four infants and toddlers all together in the same room, ages 6 weeks to 24 months. The ratio of adult to child was 1:4, with six adults available at all times. The room was well stocked with an assortment of toys and equipment for the various ages, even boasting a toddler-sized carpeted climbing structure complete with an enticing wide slide. There were plenty of soft elements in the room, like fabric-covered cushions, a couch, hanging plants, and soothing music. An interesting feature was the large full-length window facing the front garden area, giving children a view out to the world to watch people come and go from the center. Infants took their naps and played on the floor in a fenced-off area within the room to keep them safe from active toddlers. Outside, the play yard was well stocked, but it was extremely large, over-sized actually, making it very difficult for caregivers to supervise the children. The toddlers would run to the outer reaches of the yard, and the caregivers had to dash after them, trying desperately to radiate a zone of safety among all the toddlers. In this kind of setting, they had to primarily react, intervening in misbehavior rather than acting as facilitators of developmentally appropriate play.

7. Limit-setting practices

When Ethan bit his classmates, caregivers admonished him, saying something like, "No biting, Ethan. How would you like it if they did that to you? Stop that right now! You need to be nice to your friends." If they caught him in an attempt to bite before he actually did the deed, they would quickly try to redirect him, relieved that they had averted disaster. Ethan didn't receive any real consequence or guidance, though; life just went on. During my observation, the teachers had gathered the children for a snack outside and asked the children to sit in a circle. At one point, Ethan leaned over calmly with his mouth parted open, a definite plan to bite his neighbor in a "preemptive strike," as if he knew she would be too close for his comfort. The caregiver saw it, reached over and put her hand in between the children to stop the bite and then passed them the food. That was it, no further discussion, no new lessons learned.

Action Plan Worksheet		
Child's Name: Ethan		**Child's Age:** 18 months
7 Questions	**Describe the Situation**	**Design the Solutions**
1. Stage of Development	▪ Exuberant and outgoing ▪ Confused about his feelings. ▪ Doesn't understand others' feelings or need for boundaries with people. ▪ Egocentric point of view	▪ Describe his feelings; provide him with specific, useful words. ▪ Describe how other people feel. ▪ Interpret what is going on; comment on the play. ▪ Promote and demonstrate waiting and turn-taking behavior.
2. Past Experiences and Recent Changes	▪ Physically rough play with the dog is encouraged at home and confuses the issue of boundaries. ▪ Dad plays biting games with him, confusing Ethan about the issue.	▪ Curtail physical, rough play at home with the dog until Ethan's biting problem ends at the center. ▪ No more biting games, period
3. Verbal Skills	▪ Many ear infections have delayed his verbal skills. ▪ He doesn't have words for his feelings.	▪ Be a good model. Teach him to begin using short, two-word phrases as verbal tools, such as "My turn?" or "Be careful" or "I need" or "That's mine." ▪ Be a good model of sentence composition. Use "self-talk" to describe your actions during daily activities. "Look, I'm going to wipe up the water I spilled on the floor." ▪ Extend his language when he uses one-word sentences. When he says, "More," say, "Sounds like you want some more of these crunchy crackers. Here you go!" ▪ Read books to build his vocabulary and talk about what the characters are feeling. ▪ Reflect his feelings: "You're feeling mad, aren't you?"

Action Plan Worksheet (continued)		
7 Questions	**Describe the Situation**	**Design the Solutions**
4. Physical Condition	▪ An early napper, he wakes up earlier than the others and he is extremely hungry, but must wait for snack time. Prone to biting at that time	▪ Provide a snack for him upon waking.
5. Temper-ament	▪ Ethan has a fairly easy-going temperament, although he is persistent, intense, and highly active. His impatience can exhibit itself in strong, loud ways; sometimes leads to biting.	▪ Stay calm, use active listening, and provide clear explanation. Say, "I know how much you want me to play with you right now, but my hands are busy fixing lunch. I'll be over in about five minutes." ▪ Give plenty of opportunities for active play, indoors and outdoors. Afterward, help him calm down again with soft music, slow dancing, play dough, books, etc.
6. Physical Environment	▪ Biting often happens at snack time, where too many children sit at crowded round tables. ▪ Over-sized yard makes adequate supervision difficult.	▪ Use a square table for Ethan, providing corners, distance, and more well-defined personal space. ▪ Divide up the yard into two yards, with some type of fencing, to create more manageable supervision areas.
7. Limit Setting	▪ Parents and caregivers are leaving out key components in teaching Ethan alternatives to biting.	▪ Use Instructive Intervention consistently, whether he completes a bite or just attempts to bite. Proactively teach him alternatives to biting and positive ways to interact with people.

Summary

Ethan was biting for a number of reasons, all of them relatively easy to fix. He was definitely getting mixed messages about the appropriateness of his behavior. At home it was seen as funny to put your teeth on people in a playful manner. His parents had played that game with Ethan since he was a little baby. They thought he understood it was only a game, yet he was being confused. At child care playing biting games was frowned upon, to say the least.

At home it was okay to play in a physical and rough way with his big dog and with his dad, too. In fact, Ethan got strong positive feedback for acting like a little "tank" at home, because it was really entertaining for the adults. Hitting, bumping, and pushing people as a style of play was accepted and encouraged there. But at child care Ethan was instructed to be gentle and nice to people, a direct contradiction.

Much of Ethan's biting happened in the play yard. If the child care program was amenable to it, some fairly easy changes could be made to help solve that problem. Other times biting was happening at snack times or prior to snack times. Again, situations could be improved by accommodating his needs differently. Also, caregivers were leaving out some key components in teaching Ethan alternatives to biting. With collaboration between home and child care, Ethan's biting could become a thing of the past.

Conclusion

The caregivers and Ethan's parents followed the plan carefully. Everyone was motivated to be able to keep Ethan at the center. They immediately changed the way they were interacting with Ethan. Caregivers made all of the recommended changes to the environment. Within a few short days, the biting ended. Over the next few weeks, Ethan learned new verbal skills to express himself and deal with his frustration. He also learned to respect the boundaries between himself and others. As his language increased, his impulse control increased, too.

Sophia, 21 Months Old

Bad Habits, Challenging Temperament, and Boring Toys

Background

Sophia's parents reached out for professional help when the child care center gave them an ultimatum: their daughter had to stop biting other children or she would be "dismissed." Sophia had been attending the center ten hours per day for the past year. Her family had developed a good relationship with the program. When Sophia turned 18 months, she suddenly began biting on a regular basis. Once she even bit a caregiver. The director thought Sophia might be frustrated by being in a room with many babies so, as soon as a space opened up, she moved her into the older toddler class. Unfortunately, the biting continued there, too. According to incident reports Sophia's biting was "unprovoked," meaning no one could find the cause for her biting. She was extremely verbal for her age and expressed her needs perfectly well. Interestingly, biting often happened on the playground.

Sophia lived with her parents and her seven-year-old brother. Both parents worked full time as busy executives. They were a happy couple, committed to sharing parenting responsibilities and creating a pleasant home environment. They were open to learning everything they could to further develop their parenting abilities, especially as they related to Sophia's struggles. The parents found Sophia to be a more difficult-to-raise child than their firstborn. Though Sophia had never bitten her parents, she occasionally bit her brother.

Observation and Interview Results

1. Stage of development

Sophia was tall for her age and well coordinated with no physical problems except for the occasional head cold. She never had any real separation issues, attending child care easily without crying or anxiety when she was dropped off in the morning. Of course, Sophia had her share of temper tantrums, typical of an egocentric toddler. She would grab items that she wanted from her brother or from her peers. She loved spending time around adults, conversing with them easily by using full sentences at an early age. Her cognitive development was quite advanced. She could easily understand concepts at the level of a mature two-year-old.

2. Past experiences and recent changes

During the past year Sophia had been bitten several times by other toddlers in the program, an average amount and not an unusual occurrence in an ordinary toddler program. The bites took place both indoors and outside, usually over grabbing of items or territorial disputes. At home her brother teased her fairly regularly, and she had resorted to biting him as a result. He would push or hit her sometimes but he never bit her back.

Sophia was currently being weaned from the bottle. She was down to two bottles a day, one in the morning and another before bedtime. Though she generally liked taking naps, she hadn't been able to sleep at the child care program because of the new room changes. Children in the older toddler room didn't use cribs. They used floor mats instead, which were new to Sophia. Sometimes, at the beginning of naptime children moved around a bit while getting settled down on their mats. Teachers typically sat down in between the mats of the children, rubbing their backs to get them to sleep, but two adults couldn't be everywhere at once. The first hour was chaotic. (One teacher always stepped out of the room to go on lunch break at naptime, so supervision always went from three adults down to two.) Sophia appeared nervous with other children getting up and down, sometimes walking close to her in the dimmed room. She kept an eye out for them rather than let herself fall asleep. Coping without biting was more difficult for her during the afternoons in which Sophia hadn't slept at all.

3. Verbal skills

Sophia's verbal skills were advanced for her age—she was already talking in complete sentences. Because of her height, the caregivers said they "sometimes found it hard to remember how young she really was." Emotionally, however, she was still very much a toddler even though she interacted verbally like a two-year-old and was as tall.

4. Health and physical condition

Her physical condition was normal in every way. She took her teething pain in stride. She got hungry at the same times each day and liked routine mealtimes, becoming agitated if lunch or dinner were running late.

5. Temperament traits

Sophia's parents described her as prickly in terms of how she experienced her world. Sophia's mom saw her temperament as much like her own: high activity level, somewhat distractible, initially uncomfortable in new situations, not very adaptable to changes, and easily bothered by sensory experiences. There was never a doubt about how Sophia felt about anything. She expressed herself, happy or sad, in a very intense manner. She also had a high need for regularity and predictability and was persistent in what she wanted. When there was even a minor change to the normal routine, however, she became much more fussy and oppositional. Her style of play showed a strong interest in order, sorting things and lining up toys and puzzle pieces as she played with them.

6. Physical environment

In the mixed-age room of twelve infants and toddlers, the six toddlers had only a minimal assortment of simple items from which to choose. Sophia had grown bored with the choices as she matured. Even in her current classroom of twelve toddlers, the environment did not include enough sophisticated toys or small motor materials. Puzzles, books, and small manipulative building toys were in short supply. The large motor play items were mainly stuffed animals, large cardboard blocks, balls, push cars, and riding toys. Art, primarily easel painting, was only put out twice a week. Even though play dough was put out during free play time, the dough was old, dried out, and stiff.

In the play yard, there was a sandbox with few sand toys and no water nearby to use in making more complex sand structures. There was an empty water table that the caregivers used only in the summer. A plastic climbing structure resided in the corner, including a popular swing that a caregiver stood behind, pushing one lucky toddler at a time. There was a small patch of grass where children and caregivers could sit and look at books or have a circle time. Asphalt offered a hard surface on which to use the riding toys and kick the balls. All in all, the environment was lacking in complexity and did not have enough play spaces for twelve children, indoors or outdoors.

7. Limit-setting practices

Sophia's parents used time-outs as their discipline strategy: one minute of time for every year of life. When Sophia bit her brother, they put her in a time-out location in the kitchen. Afterward, they made her apologize to her brother before she could play again. Sophia didn't mind time-out at all and would giggle on her way to the time-out spot. In fact, lately, Sophia would bite her brother then immediately yell, "Sorry, Mommy!" and willingly walk over and plop down in the time-out spot to wait for her mother.

At child care there had been some recent turnover in staff. There were inconsistencies in how the caregivers handled misbehavior. Children received mixed messages depending on who stepped in to deal with the conflict. Since Sophia didn't seem to mind being on time-out in the classroom, the staff had started sending her to the director's office when she bit, to remove her from the room altogether. They equated their strategy to that of an elementary school child's experience of going to the principal's office. (If this didn't work, they planned to send her home after every bite.) Sending her to the office did not have the desired effect at all; Sophia loved being with adults. For her, leaving the classroom was like having a break. She found it interesting to watch what went on in the office where she would get a new kind of attention from a new set of adults.

Summary

Sophia was capable of responding verbally to her peers when she was upset. She bit people because other stressors were inhibiting her ability to use those skills and because there was ineffective limit setting at home. Sophia had some temperament traits that made her more easily upset by certain aspects of the environment, things that could be changed by her caregivers. Also, she was faced with spending an entire day in an environment that didn't stimulate and challenge her, making it hard for her to find activities that kept her productively engaged.

Action Plan Worksheet		
Child's Name: Sophia		Child's Age: 21 months
7 Questions	**Describe the Situation**	**Design the Solutions**
1. Stage of Development	• Confused about her own feelings. • Doesn't understand others' feelings. • Egocentric point of view • Impulsively grabs toys from children. • Her cognitive level is advanced; adults forget she's just a toddler.	• Describe her feelings; provide her with specific, useful words. • Describe how other people feel. • Interpret what is going on; comment on the play. • Promote and demonstrate turn-taking behavior. • Remember that she needs more help than it appears.

2. Past Experiences and Recent Changes	• Sophia was bitten several times by other toddlers.
	• Grabs items from her seven-year-old brother successfully.
	• Sophia's brother teases her, occasionally grabs things, and hits her, provoking biting.
	
	• Recently moved into the "older toddler room."
	
	• In the process of being weaned from the bottle. No bottles allowed in this classroom.
	• Must use a nap mat now instead of a crib.
		• Utilize better techniques with everyone in the center.
		• Parents need to follow through to set limits on grabbing from brother.
		• Teach Sophia's brother new turn-taking strategies:
		  ▸ Establish a time frame for waiting. Set a timer for use of certain popular items.
		  ▸ Teach her to ask him, "Be done in five minutes?" instead of grabbing. Model this for them both.
		• Be patient; recognize that it takes more time for a child with this type of temperament to adjust.
		• Continue to work towards weaning at home, too. Offer a washcloth or teething toy when tense.
		• Sit nearby and calm her at the beginning of naptime rather than wait until she is more upset. Consider schedule changes to insure enough staff at the beginning of nap.

3. Verbal Skills	• Sophia is a toddler who talks in complete sentences, so teachers expect too much grown-up behavior from her. They don't realize how frustrated she is that the other toddlers can't communicate with her. • She doesn't use words to express her feelings; she gives in to impulses under stress.	• Don't just say "use your words." Encourage her to use specific phrases, verbal tools, such as "May I have a turn?" or "Move back" or "I want that" or "That's my chair," etc. Help others do the same. • Read books to her to build up her vocabulary and talk about what the characters are feeling.

Action Plan Worksheet (continued)		
7 Questions	**Describe the Situation**	**Design the Solutions**
4. Physical Condition	■ Gets very agitated when she's hungry and always gets hungry at the same time of day. ■ Needs a daily nap; gets extremely fussy and more prone to biting on afternoons she doesn't sleep.	■ Be mindful of this susceptibility and stick to the meal schedule as much as possible. Provide snacks when running late. ■ Find ways to help her calm down, such as rubbing her back, and put her in the most nondistracting location possible within the nap room. Make sure she has a lovey to sleep with for self-comforting.
5. Temperament	■ Sophia has many challenging traits. She is extremely persistent in what she wants and she voices her feelings in a loud, intense manner. ■ Low sensory threshold. Having children rush around or crowd her makes her anxious, and she acts out. ■ She is nonadaptable; change is hard for her. ■ Sophia is distractible and finds it hard to pay close attention when adults talk to her about behavior.	■ Stay calm, use active listening, and provide clear explanation. Say, "I know how much you want me to help you right now, but my hands are busy putting clothes in the washer. I'll be over in about five minutes." ■ Help her physically during transitions. Hold her hand, walk with her, and get her engaged in play. ■ Give her advanced notice before changes. Say, "In five minutes, we'll be getting washed up for lunch. You can paint more again after naptime." ■ Use anchoring to keep her attention on you. Bend down, place your hand gently on her shoulder or arm, and use eye contact. Speak softly.
6. Physical Environment	■ Aimless wandering; lack of stimulating materials. She is mainly interested in small motor play but most items in the classroom are for gross motor play or for infants. ■ There are too few play spaces overall.	■ Purchase more developmentally appropriate items: dolls and accessories, water table toys, fat chalk, sand box props, play dough, books, peg boards, shape sorters, blocks, and puzzles. ■ Make sure to set out enough activities for the group size.
7. Limit Setting	■ Time-out is seen as a game. ■ She loves going to the office after biting. ■ Apologies have become an easy way out of trouble. ■ Adults are not providing clear instruction.	■ Discontinue ineffectual time-outs. ■ Stop taking her down to the office when she bites. ■ Stop making her apologize, both at home and at the center. Instead, ask her, "Are you all finished biting?" ■ Use Instructive Intervention consistently, whether she completed a bite or just attempted to bite. Teach her alternatives to biting and positive ways to interact.

Conclusion

Sophie's parents and the child care program committed to the Action Plan we developed in every way. The director of the program made significant improvements to the environment by investing in additional age-appropriate materials. She also met with the caregivers individually to work with them on responding more effectively to misbehavior, role playing new responses in several types of situations. The caregivers even kept note cards in their pockets for the first week to keep themselves "on message" while they learned their new responses. With such consistent intervention in addition to environmental changes, within a week the biting had ended. Sophia really liked the verbal tools she was given to use in times of distress, ways to express her anger and to get the caregiver's attention. She even started asking, "How many minutes?" to the caregivers when she wanted a turn with the swing. She seemed to draw comfort from the fact that there was a finite time to wait for popular things. Knowing the number of minutes made the wait much more endurable.

At home Sophia's parents limited her brother's teasing and discontinued using time-out with her. No longer did she get away with a meaningless apology. Her parents continued to learn more techniques to help Sophia and her brother resolve conflicts. Sophia continued to be a temperamentally challenging child, but her parents became quite expert at reading her needs and creating an environment that was a good fit for her, so Sophia flourished.

Lukas, 22 Months Old

Bottles, Blame, and Boredom

Background

Lukas's mother went back to work full time when Lukas was four months old. She found a family child care home near her house, and Lukas was happy there. When he was 12 months old, a space opened up at the child care center sponsored by his mom's company, so she signed up and enrolled him in the toddler room. This arrangement was very convenient for her, and Lukas seemed to really like the larger space and wider range of play activities. Then, when he turned 22 months old, he was moved up early into the two-year-old room.

One day Lukas's mom got a report from his caregiver that he bit another child in his group. She immediately phoned Lukas's pediatrician, who assured her that this was normal behavior for a toddler and that the child care staff should be able to handle it easily. Each day, however, the caregivers reported several biting episodes. These always took place in the morning and always outside on the playground. Lukas's parents became very defensive, convinced that Lukas had learned this behavior at the center. They simply couldn't understand why the teachers didn't intervene in time. The doctor had said biting was normal, but the child care staff seemed unable to stop it from happening. Communications became very strained between the mother and the center. After about a month of this, the parents were informed that they should begin looking for alternate placement. The next day, after Lukas bit the daughter of his mom's colleague, Lukas's mom reached out for professional help.

Observation and Interview Results

1. Stage of development

Lukas was a healthy, average-sized toddler. He often had some difficulty in separating from his mother in the mornings, but after she left he happily settled in to play with his favorite toys. He had a strong preference for toys with small pieces, such as manipulatives, rather than large motor toys, such as bikes and balls. Most of the time he played comfortably alongside other children in parallel play, as would be expected of a toddler.

2. Past experiences and recent changes

Lukas had never been bitten at home or at child care, though he had seen other people getting bitten. Recently, Lukas's dad had begun traveling frequently for his job, sometimes being gone for two weeks at a time. Lukas's mom didn't like to be alone at night, so she let Lukas stay up late watching television with her. She rationalized it by saying that he got plenty of sleep since he napped every afternoon at the child care center. Another recent change for Lukas was that he used to drink a full bottle in the toddler room twice a day. Now that he was in the two-year-old room, though, he had to abide by the no-bottle policy.

3. Verbal skills

Lukas had limited verbal skills. While he could understand adults and comply with their requests, he had a hard time making his own needs known. His speech was very unclear, hard to decipher by adults and children alike, and he stuttered occasionally.

4. Health and physical condition

Lukas had never had an ear infection and appeared to have no hearing problems. His teething patterns were normal, coming and going with typical eruptions. He ate breakfast in the morning at the child care program and always ate a big lunch. He was an oral child, often putting his fingers in his mouth during the day. Lukas was typically exhausted by naptime, falling asleep as soon as he lay down, napping for two and one-half hours each day.

5. Temperament traits

Lukas was a fairly sedentary child. He didn't like climbing and running. He was more content to sit and look at books, use paints, or play with peg boards and puzzles. He didn't show much facial emotion, making him hard for people to interpret. He was described as a mostly serious child, not exactly negative but not positive, either.

6. Physical environment

The two-year-old classroom was a comfortable and soothing yet stimulating place to spend time in. It was adequately sized and rich in a wide variety of age-appropriate and challenging materials. By contrast, the playground was not well equipped. There were not enough play spaces and no variety. There were no small motor activities set up to augment the large motor items. The playground consisted mainly of a large climbing structure on a rubber mat, assorted riding toys, and a large sandbox. There were no benches on which adults or children could sit. There were no painting easels or chalk drawing areas. There wasn't any grass for relaxing in the shade to look at books or play with dolls. There weren't any tables set up for playing with bubble-making fluids or for building with small blocks. All in all, the playground was sparsely furnished.

7. Limit-setting practices

At home Lukas ruled the roost. He was the only child of two older parents. His parents were particularly uncomfortable when people expressed upsetting feelings. They were opposed to any kind of confrontation, so they let Lukas do as he pleased around the house. Their solution to any kind of fussy behavior was to offer him a bottle so he would calm down. They reported giving Lukas an average of eight bottles per day on the weekends and two or three bottles on weekday evenings.

Lukas's parents had no idea what to do on the home front regarding biting since he never bit them. When they got him home in the evening, they tried to reason with him, asking him to be nice to his friends, saying it "made Mommy sad when he bit people."

At the child care program, the current staff had various levels of expertise in handling misbehavior and were inconsistent in how they responded. Children got mixed messages, depending on who stepped in to deal with the conflict. The staff used a mixture of lecturing and scolding Lukas when he bit someone. Lately, the teachers had started taking him to the director's office when he bit another child, saying, "It's not nice to bite people, Lukas. You have to sit here and think about that." This approach did not have the desired effect.

Summary

Lukas's biting happened as a result of things adults were doing at home and in the child care center. For months he had been allowed to constantly use a bottle to relieve any type of stress at home. This created a tendency for him to respond to daily stressors orally through biting. He has not been learning any other means of dealing with life other than to block it out with a bottle. At child care, Lukas has been using bottles to soothe himself orally when feeling fussy or tired for nearly two years. When transferred to the two-year-old room, he immediately had to give up all daytime bottles, leaving him at a loss in dealing with stress, frustration, or disappointment. He started biting soon after this major change.

Lukas's verbal skills were minimal, partially due to lack of rich language experiences offered at home and at the center. Also, given the current limit-setting practices provided by his caregivers, he wasn't learning any new skills or language for dealing with frustration. His biting occurred only in the morning on the playground where play materials were inadequate.

Action Plan Worksheet		
Child's Name: Lukas		Child's Age: 22 months
7 Questions	**Describe the Situation**	**Design the Solutions**
1. Stage of Development	▪ Confused about his own and other people's feelings. ▪ Egocentric point of view ▪ Impulsively grabs toys from children.	▪ Describe his feelings; provide him with specific, useful words. Promote empathy for other people. ▪ Interpret what is going on; comment on the play. ▪ Promote and demonstrate turn-taking behavior.
2. Past Experiences and Recent Changes	▪ Lukas hasn't been bitten by another child but has seen others getting bitten. ▪ Lukas just moved into the two-year-old room where they don't allow any bottles, after having two bottles per day in the toddler room. Lukas is a very oral child, always wanting something in his mouth. ▪ He gets an excessive number of bottles at home in the evenings and weekends.	▪ When biting happens to others, remember that all children are learning by watching the adult's reaction and proposed solution. ▪ Give him access to cool washcloths, teething toys, and sippy cups. ▪ Start weaning Lukas from these bottles over the next couple of weeks. Introduce a lovey to help him self-soothe. Stay warm and firm.

(Continued on next page)

Action Plan Worksheet (continued)		
7 Questions	**Describe the Situation**	**Design the Solutions**
3. Verbal Skills	▪ Lukas has very limited verbal skills. He can hear and understand others but has trouble making his needs understood. His speech is unclear and he sometimes stutters. ▪ He doesn't use words to express himself but gives in to impulses to bite when under stress.	▪ Be a good model of sentence composition. Use self-talk to describe your actions during daily activities. "I'm going to fold all these towels and make a pile right here." ▪ Extend his language when he uses one-word sentences. When he says, "Dat," say, "Sounds like you want to wear that warm red coat." ▪ Don't just say "use your words." Encourage him to use specific phrases, verbal tools, such as "May I have a turn?" or "Get away" or "I want that" or "That's my chair," etc. Help others do the same. ▪ Read books to him to build up his vocabulary and let him hear the flow of language. Pause at times and talk about what the characters are feeling and doing.
4. Physical Condition	▪ Lukas is consistently fatigued at school in the mornings. He never gets enough sleep at home; his mom lets him stay up to keep her company until 10:30 P.M. because his dad travels often.	▪ Lukas's mom needs to create a healthy bedtime routine for Lukas and stick to it. She should consult with a parent educator, if needed, to help her deal with separation issues and bedtime techniques.
5. Temper- ament	▪ Even though he regularly bites, Lukas's temperament is calm, serious, persistent, low intensity, and nonadaptable.	▪ Adults need to be prepared to outlast Lukas's insistence when demanding a bottle or toy, especially his mom, who is inclined to cave in when faced with disharmony. Use active listening and redirection.
6. Physical Environment	▪ Lukas only bites outside. The playground is lacking in activities that he likes. All items in the yard are for gross motor play: running, climbing, riding, etc. ▪ Too few play spaces overall	▪ Bring out small motor and creative activities: water table/bubbles, a table, a mat for block building or reading, shade umbrella, places to sit, water painting on sidewalk, etc. ▪ Make sure to set out enough activities to accommodate the group.

Action Plan Worksheet (continued)		
7 Questions	**Describe the Situation**	**Design the Solutions**
7. Limit Setting	▪ Parents are averse to all conflict. ▪ Parents and teachers are not providing clear messages or instruction.	▪ Parents need to set limits in ways that are not tentative or apologetic. Anticipate oppositional behavior during typical limit-testing periods. Take a parent education course. ▪ Use Instructive Intervention consistently, whether he completed a bite or attempted one. Teach him alternatives to biting and positive ways to interact.

Conclusion

The staff at the child care center had not known that Lukas was getting eight bottles a day on the weekends. The parents had not seen the connection between non-stop bottles at home and Lukas's dealing with stress at child care through oral means such as biting. As soon as both parties understood this fact, they began a fruitful conversation about ways in which they could help Lukas with weaning and in learning verbal tools and self-comforting techniques to replace his bottle habit. The parents stopped blaming the center for Lukas's biting. The center purchased some new items for the playground that benefited all of the two-year-olds. The teachers began using the new, clear responses to biting and attempts at biting. They found this problem-solving method useful for all sorts of conflicts on the playground and in the classroom. Lukas's parents continued in parent education so they could learn how to set limits without being nervous or apologetic. Before too long Lukas's biting was a thing of the past.

Abigail, Two Years Old

Divorce, Negative Attention, and Family Day Care Dynamics

Background

Abigail spent her days in a family child care home that included one caregiver and six children, a combination of infants, toddlers, and Abigail, the only two-year-old. It was generally a happy little family setting. Abigail's mother was thrilled to have found Gina to be such a kind and loving caregiver.

Seven months ago, Abigail started having trouble with jealousy. She got very angry when the caregiver paid attention to the other children. She bit or attempted to bite someone on a daily basis, whether provoked or unprovoked. She never seemed to feel remorseful afterward. Quite the opposite, in fact, she would even talk casually about biting in the car on the way to child care. She would use biting to successfully get negative attention, both morning and afternoon. And, after a biting incident, she had a regular routine. She would immediately smile, lean over the victim, say, "Want some ice?" and open the freezer door to get the ice. Then she would bring it to the child, saying "I'm sorry," while holding the ice on the victim's arm.

Biting was becoming a constant, and Gina took a stand. While it disappointed her to lose Abigail, she couldn't allow Abigail to inflict so much pain on the other children and endanger her business. An ultimatum was given, and the countdown began: two weeks to find a solution or else find a new caregiver.

Observation and Interview Results

1. Stage of development

Abigail was extremely coordinated, even courageous about physical challenges such as climbing, running, and tumbling. As the oldest of the group by quite a bit, there was no other child who was a good playmate for her, no one to help her learn more mature social skills.

2. Past experiences and recent changes

Abigail never bit any adults; nor did she bite anywhere other than at her child care home. She had been bitten in the past by another child there, but that child had moved on to go to a preschool.

A few months earlier she had finished potty training, and that had gone smoothly as she was very motivated to see herself as a "big girl." Now her parents wanted to wean her from the pacifier, so they stopped sending it to child care. She only got to use it at home. But the biggest stress was the change caused by her parents' recent divorce, ending in a joint custody arrangement that created several transitions for Abigail over the course of each week. Unfortunately, her parents were not acting very kind to each other. They tried not to argue in front of Abigail, but she sensed the tension between them.

3. Verbal skills

Abigail was extremely bright and very verbal. She was speaking in full sentences by the age of 18 months.

4. Physical condition

Abigail was in good physical condition, having had no ear infections and very few colds. She was a picky eater, in line with her temperament, and it was hard for her parents to find much variety for her diet. She mainly ate simple finger foods like peanut butter and jelly sandwiches, pancakes, and cheese cubes. She had difficulty falling asleep, rocking back and forth, rubbing her hair, and talking to herself before calming down. She had been weaned from the bottle quickly, but still drank a bottle at night while sitting in the rocking chair with her mom or dad.

5. Temperament traits

Abigail had a challenging temperament. She was known as "the prickly pear." Her activity level was very high. She was acutely sensitive to touch, sounds, tastes, smells, and visual clutter. She tore off wet clothes immediately, a tendency that made potty training easy. Abigail was incredibly persistent and had a high need for order and regularity. This was reflected in a purposeful style to her play, through lining random items up in a certain order or arranging the blocks and the doll family in a specific way. Unfortunately, whenever younger toddlers came barreling though the playroom, Abigail's set-ups frequently got ruined, adding to her frustration and urge to bite.

6. Physical environment

The child care home was well set up to care for a small group of mixed-age children. There was a large family room full of toys off the kitchen. The family room opened up to a big backyard with a sandbox, water table, climbing structure, grass, and shade. Gina had set up a nice assortment of loose parts, such as riding toys, balls, paint easels, and digging tools. One problem with the environment was that Gina didn't have any play space to set the infants where they could be safe from the older children, especially Abigail. Gina didn't believe in playpens, "too much like a little jail," so she always carried the babies with her during the day or stayed near their infant seats, unless they were sleeping. As a result, it was hard for the toddlers to ever get Gina's full attention. Lack of storage was another problem in this environment. Toys ended up scattered all over the floor, creating a haphazard feel to the area and making it frustrating for children to find things and have organized play times.

7. Limit setting

Gina wanted Abigail to feel some consequence after misbehaving through biting. Whenever Abigail bit one of the children, Gina instructed her to get some ice to make the other child feel better. She told Abigail that "it wasn't nice to bite" and implored her to stop because "it made Gina sad." At home Abigail's mom and dad were very lax in setting consistent limits, frequently giving in to tantrums in order to stop the whining or crying.

Summary

Many factors were contributing to Abigail's behavior problems. She was temperamentally very sensitive to the clutter and congestion in her play space, which caused her unnecessary agitation. And as a highly active child, she needed to have her energy channeled in appropriate ways. Being the oldest, Abigail was expected to entertain herself much of the time. Her hurtful behavior at child care was directly related to feeling a lack of attention. For a two-year-old child, it was typical to be impatient and lack impulse control. Also, Abigail's parents were exacerbating the situation. At home they jumped to please her when she demanded attention, no matter what they were currently doing. Even though she was a verbal child, she hadn't learned any helpful, specific phrases for expressing her strong feelings and desires.

Abigail's trouble with sleeping contributed to her lack of patience with others because she was often tired. In addition, getting ice for the victim, the "consequence" for her biting, had become a fun part of the process for Abigail, a motivating factor in itself. And finally, Abigail had begun to experience general feelings of insecurity and tension based on the changes in her lifestyle due to her parents' divorce.

Action Plan Worksheet		
Child's Name: Abigail		Child's Age: 2 years
7 Questions	**Describe the Situation**	**Design the Solutions**
1. Stage of Development	■ Egocentric point of view ■ She has no peers at child care to help her learn new social skills.	■ Promote empathy and compassion for other people. Comment on what is happening during play and what other people might be feeling. When reading books, talk about what the characters are feeling. ■ Look for other playmates her age when going to the neighborhood playground, etc.
2. Past Experiences and Recent Changes	■ She only bites at child care. She has been bitten herself by a child who no longer goes to this child care program. ■ Abigail is being weaned from the pacifier, only getting it at home now. ■ Her parents are newly separated with a joint custody arrangement.	■ Focus on key changes to make at child care. And remember, what happens at home always impacts a child's ability to cope with stressors at the child care program, too. ■ Offer Abigail something else to chew on at child care as needed. ■ Parents need to make sure they spend uninterrupted playtime with her before bedtime, providing satisfying personal attention.

Action Plan Worksheet (continued)		
7 Questions	**Describe the Situation**	**Design the Solutions**
3. Verbal Skills	▪ Abigail is extremely verbal for her age and able to express herself in complete sentences. ▪ She isn't using her verbal skills in times of stress.	▪ Don't forget that she is only two years old. Her language gives the impression she is more socially mature than she really is. ▪ Encourage her to use short, specific phrases as verbal tools when she gets upset, such as "May I have a turn?" or "Move away" or "I need a turn" or "That's my chair," etc.
4. Physical Condition	▪ Abigail has trouble falling asleep at naptime and bedtime. She is being weaned from her bottle, only getting one at nighttime now. When she is not well rested, she is more apt to act out against the children.	▪ Begin to include a lovey and some music to the nighttime rocking chair ritual so that she can be weaned off the bottle soon. Adding other sleep cues always helps when taking away old ones. A good lovey will become an important transition object between her parents' two homes.
5. Temper-ament	▪ Abigail's temperament exhibits several traits in the extreme: high activity, high sensory awareness, very persistent, nonadaptable, and a high need for regularity. ▪ She can easily feel cramped by the other children, becoming tense and overwhelmed. ▪ It is very hard for her to wait for things or to feel comfortable with a change in the daily routine.	▪ While it is difficult for Gina to take Abigail outside often to drain off her high energy, she can put on bouncy dance music and give Abigail scarves to dance with. ▪ Knowing that close interactions are especially hard for Abigail, Gina can sometimes arrange a separate play space for Abigail, such as sitting up at the table or counter to play. ▪ Encourage her to express herself when feeling tense or upset. Teach her to say, "I need more space. Can you move over?" or "When is it my turn?"
6. Physical Environment	▪ No safe place to set the infants where the toddlers/twos can't harm them ▪ Lack of storage for toys ▪ Insufficient toys for two-year-olds	▪ Create a safe zone for the infants with baby gates, accordion fencing, an inflatable pool, carpeted boxes, etc. ▪ Add open shelving and bins for toys. ▪ Purchase stimulating and challenging toys for two-year-olds.
7. Limit Setting	▪ Parents give in to tantrums. ▪ Ice/apology for bites not working. ▪ Adults are not providing clear messages or instruction.	▪ Do not cave in; stay warm and firm. ▪ No more ice or apologies ▪ Use Instructive Intervention consistently, whether she completed a bite or attempted one. Teach her alternatives to biting and positive ways to interact.

Conclusion

Even though the relationship between the parents did not improve greatly (and they did not go to a counselor, as suggested), Abigail stopped biting altogether within a couple of weeks after changes had been implemented. As soon as Gina stopped allowing Abigail the fun of fetching ice for her biting victims, much of the motivation for Abigail's biting disappeared. Abigail received less negative attention and began to receive attention in more positive ways. She began using the suggested verbal phrases when feeling crowded by the younger children and was successful in venting her feelings without resorting to biting.

Gina set up the child care family room differently, using the suggestions from the plan. She noticed a tremendous difference in her own comfort level and in the way the children played in the same space without infringing on each others' needs. Also, the two-year-old materials she added to her program kept Abigail engaged in play longer on her own, enjoying new age-appropriate challenges.

Abigail's parents and Gina were grateful to learn more about how Abigail's temperament affected her view of the world and how she interpreted interactions with children and adults. They limited her ability to manipulate the situation and began using new ways to assist her in getting through stressful situations, while teaching her patience and impulse control. Abigail continued another year in this home-based program before starting preschool as a four-year-old.

Jayden, Three Years Old

Social Inexperience, Speech Problems, and Sibling Issues

Background

Jayden was the middle child in the family. He had a six-month-old baby brother and an eight-year-old sister. Jayden's baby brother had been born prematurely with multiple physical problems that had created a stressful time for the whole family while the baby was in and out of the hospital. The baby was better now, but things had been tense for several months. Jayden's grandma had been the main caregiver during the first three years of his life. Jayden's parents both worked full time and Grandma had to focus on the baby, so Jayden was enrolled at the neighborhood preschool and child care center. Unfortunately, after just a few weeks of attendance he had developed a reputation for himself as the classroom bully.

Jayden was a physically active child who expressed his emotions in a very strong and exuberant way, whether happy or sad. He enjoyed playing with other children his own age, but he had trouble communicating with them due to his immature speech and language skills. In fact, usually adults had trouble understanding what Jayden was trying to say, especially when he was upset. When he became frustrated, Jayden had a tendency to whine and often strike out through hitting children or adults, especially if he felt his requests were being ignored. The preschool director wanted to be able to keep him at the school but only if his behavior improved right away.

Observation and Interview Results

1. Stage of development

Jayden was not used to being around children his own age, but he didn't seem uncomfortable around them. He happily played near other children and liked showing them his paintings, block buildings, etc. When they didn't respond to him *immediately,* he became confused and impatient. Sometimes this feeling turned into anger if he felt ignored.

2. Past experiences and recent changes

At home Jayden liked to play with his older sister Dina, but she didn't have much interest or patience in spending time with him. She really knew what would upset him, however, and she teased him quite a bit. She was much more interested in holding and entertaining the new baby than in playing with Jayden and he knew it.

The past six months had been full of changes with the new baby and new preschool program, which meant new rules, new people, and new expectations. At school Jayden had never been physically hurt by another child.

3. Verbal skills

Jayden was quite behind in his speech and language development, with skills more like that of a toddler. He used short sentences, such as "It's my turn" or "More for me?" or "Watch me, Mommy!" He didn't have longer conversations using more complex and descriptive words like his three-year-old peers. Reportedly, adults and children alike had trouble understanding his speech more than half of the time. When adults tried to coach him on how to say certain words, he cooperated with them and tried valiantly to repeat the words to his best ability, but he was often unintelligible.

4. Physical condition

Jayden drooled and his mouth moved in a "sloppy" manner when he formed words. Also, he had battled ear infections for most of his life. His doctor had recommended that he get tubes put into his ears. This procedure was planned for the near future.

5. Temperament traits

Jayden was always on the move, bouncing around with energy in a boisterous way. He expressed himself in a strong, enthusiastic, animated way no matter what emotion he was feeling at the time. He was fairly adaptable to changes in routines, his mood was predominantly positive; he had a moderate expression of persistence and distractibility; and a moderate sensory threshold.

6. Physical environment

His home was small, but there was plenty of space to play in the living room and backyard. He and his sister had many toys. Jayden's preschool program was one of the best in the area, complete with a wide variety of materials for all skill levels and interests. His class was composed of twenty children with two teachers and an assistant teacher. The classroom was laid out thoughtfully with sufficient play spaces, pathways, and soft elements. There were duplicates of favorite items and a good balance of fine motor and large motor toys. There was a park nearby where the children went on frequent walks.

7. Limit-setting practices

Jayden's teachers in the preschool program were very knowledgeable. They utilized their classroom environment in the most optimum way and used the most appropriate type of teaching responses when Jayden hurt other children. Before dropping him off at preschool, his mom always warned Jayden not to be a "bad boy." Those were always the last words he heard her say to him.

Summary

Jayden's misbehavior stemmed from problems in several areas. Obviously, his verbal skills were delayed since he had suffered many ear infections and lack of language stimulation. It was critical for Jayden to have a speech and language evaluation to determine if there were any other developmental problems and to formulate a plan going forward. Jayden's parents did not have a good grasp on how to teach children language skills. Their best attempt was to quiz him on animal sounds, show him ABC flashcards, and park him in front of educational television shows once in a while. They needed some guidance on how to interact with him more effectively. As the middle child, Jayden had experienced a lack of individual attention due to the parents' other activities and needs. His own needs had been ignored so much, though, that he was falling behind and struggling socially. He wanted to participate positively in play with other children, but he got emotionally overwhelmed when he couldn't communicate with them and acted out in frustration. At home Jayden's sister wasn't helping matters by fanning the flames of frustration with teasing. His parents needed some ideas for changing the dynamics of social/emotional interaction within the family, and they also needed some new limit-setting techniques.

Action Plan Worksheet		
Child's Name: Jayden		Child's Age: 3 years
7 Questions	**Describe the Situation**	**Design the Solutions**
1. Stage of Development	▪ He is inexperienced around other children and becomes confused, impatient, and angry when ignored. ▪ Impulsively hits and grabs toys from children.	▪ Describe his feelings; provide him with specific, useful words. Comment on other people's feelings. Promote empathy for other people. ▪ Interpret what is going on; comment on the play. ▪ Promote and demonstrate pro-social and turn-taking behavior.
2. Past Experiences and Recent Changes	▪ Jayden's sister teases him. ▪ The past six months have been full of changes: new baby, new school, new rules, new routine, new people, etc.	▪ Parents need to set firm limits on teasing. They should set out open-ended activities at home that both ages can play with together, such as play dough, painting, dramatic play with dolls/dress-up clothes, books, dancing to music, water play, etc. ▪ Be patient with him. Give Jayden advance warnings during the day and evening prior to transitions. ▪ Parents should spend uninterrupted, individual time with Jayden as much as possible to help offset the time they must devote to the baby.

(Continued on next page)

Action Plan Worksheet (continued)		
7 Questions	Describe the Situation	Design the Solutions
3. Verbal Skills	■ Jayden's verbal skills are delayed at a toddler level. His speech is often unintelligible, especially to other children. He drools and moves his mouth in a sloppy manner.	■ Get Jayden signed up for a full speech and language evaluation. The therapist will work with him on a regular basis and will provide parents and teachers with ideas for activities that will expand his skills. ■ Be a good model of sentence composition. Use self-talk to describe your actions during daily activities. "Let's have sandwiches. First, I'll get out the bread." ■ Extend his language when he uses one-word sentences. When he says, "Mine," say, "I hear you. You want to play with the dump truck now." ■ Read books to him to build up his vocabulary and let him hear the flow of language. Pause at times and talk about what the characters are feeling and doing.
4. Physical Condition	■ Multiple ear infections have affected Jayden's hearing.	■ His doctor is planning to put tubes in Jayden's ears.
5. Temperament	■ Highly active, intense, enthusiastic, and animated ■ Adaptable to change with a moderate expression of sensory threshold, persistence, and distractibility	■ Provide lots of physical activity indoors and outdoors to help channel his energy. This may have been lacking, due to earlier babysitting arrangements with his more sedentary grandmother.
6. Physical Environment	N/A	N/A
7. Limit Setting	■ Jayden's mom always set the stage for failure by warning him not to "be a bad boy." ■ Parents don't know what to do when Jayden's sister teases him.	■ Mom should change her message by saying, "Have a fun day at school, Jayden. Remember to talk to a teacher if you feel upset about anything while playing with your friends. See you later." ■ Let her know that teasing is bullying, that it won't be tolerated, and that she could lose privileges if she continues to tease him. Follow up with consequences when she continues. ■ Encourage him to use specific phrases, verbal tools, such as "I don't like that" or "Don't tease me" or "Move away" or "Stop that" or "Be careful." ■ Use Instructive Intervention as needed.

Conclusion

Jayden started seeing a speech and language therapist on a regular basis, and his parents and grandma began using new speech and language techniques at home. They shared ideas with the teachers at school, too. Also, Jayden had tubes put in his ears to help with his ability to hear what was going on in his surroundings. Both of these changes were the main solutions to Jayden's behavior problems. His parents and caregivers followed the plan, and soon Jayden began to make better choices when he found himself in a stressful social/emotional situation.

Part IV

The Action Plan

Create Your Action Plan

It is now time to put to use all you have learned in the previous chapters as you create an Action Plan for the child in your life who bites. Observations of the child by parents and caregivers, as well as meetings among parents and caregivers, are key to gathering the information you need. The steps outlined in this chapter will help you manage the process efficiently. It is important not to shortchange this process.

Once you uncover the underlying reasons for the hurtful behavior, you can begin to make changes to the environment, the daily routine, the child's health, or your expectations where necessary. Simply relying on new, more appropriate limit-setting responses will not be sufficient. A well-constructed plan will shorten the time it takes a child who bites to deal with stressors more positively.

How to observe a child

When you observe the child, start with a completely open mind, not assuming you already know the reasons for biting. Put yourself in his or her shoes while you observe. Focus only on observing, not teaching, caring for, or intervening (if your situation allows). Use the Seven Questions to guide you in what to look for. To review briefly:

1. Developmental issues? (Page 25)
2. Past experiences or recent changes? (Page 33)
3. Verbal skills? (Page 39)
4. Child's physical condition? (Page 45)
5. Temperament? (Page 50)
6. Physical environment? (Page 62)
7. Limit-setting strategies? (Page 70)

Observing in group care

The observer should be someone who is not responsible for working with the group of children at the same time because she or he will not be able to do both. The observer will want to sit quietly out of the way on the edge of the action with a note pad. She/he will take notes on what the child says and does, and how the child behaves around the other children and caregivers. The observer must be completely focused, in a position to watch the child at play, seeing the world from the child's point of view at every moment of the observation. The observer should also make notes regarding what he or she assumes to be the child's motivations for actions or reactions to objects and people. The observer's notes will be studied later by all adults involved in creating the Action Plan. It will take about sixty to ninety minutes to do this observation.

Observing at home

Parents should try to get someone else to do the observation or, if they must do it themselves, at least do it when they can be on the sidelines just watching their child play. They may also be able to fill out some information on the Action Plan worksheet without formal observation since the smaller home setting has less complex social dynamics and a more familiar environment. Regardless, the guidelines above for observing at the early childhood program apply at home as well.

Documenting of all biting incidents

Documenting hurtful behavior is a good idea whether the child stays at home or is in a group care program. Keep track of what happened prior to the biting and note how the situation was managed. These tracking forms will suggest more clues as to the root cause of the problem. (See page 118 for Injury and Incident Report forms.)

Note: The caregiver on duty at the time the child is picked up should have a good understanding of what took place during and after the biting so that she or he can explain it to the child's parent. It is not enough to leave a cryptic note in a child's cubby for the parent to puzzle over and be alarmed by. Face-to-face conversation is necessary, even though giving and receiving this kind of information is tough, to be sure.

Working together to develop the Action Plan

Once observations have been carried out, the next step is for parents and caregivers to meet to discuss the findings. The notes that may have been made at the end of each of the Seven Questions chapters, the child's temperament profile, the observer's notes, and any other information the group may be able to share are discussed. One person in the group should be designated to write the short, concise observations and proposed solutions onto the Action Plan worksheet (pages 112–113) as the conversation leads to decisions about what to do. You may also want to use the online Action Plan form on *www.stopthefightingandbiting.com,* since it can expand as necessary to encompass your work. Also refer to the Action Plans in Part III, "Case Studies," as examples.

Sharing information with all adults involved

The completed Action Plan needs to be shared with everyone who cares for the child to ensure that all adults use the same approach to address the biting behavior. Sometimes it is advisable to have a session with caregivers to teach new skills, for example, using Instructive Intervention (page 21), performing the Puppet Show Script (page 22), teaching children the language for expressing feelings and needs or desires, devising more appropriate limit-setting strategies, and whatever else might be needed so that everyone is following the same plan.

Review progress or developments every few days. Refer often to the Action Plan to be sure the recommendations from each of the Seven Questions boxes are being implemented and nothing is forgotten. Make notes in the boxes or on the back of the Action Plan worksheet of anything relevant that the child does in his or her learning how to handle stresses without biting.

How long will this process take?

Good question. . . . Let's assume that:

1. You have created a realistic plan that takes into account all of the underlying reasons

for the child's biting behavior,

2. The child's stressors have been reduced and expectations have been adjusted to match the child's developmental capabilities,

3. During each biting attempt, parents and caregivers are consistent, firm, clear, and warm so that the child is experiencing the same message in the same manner repeatedly,

4. The child is being taught how to express feelings appropriately, and

5. The child is being given new tools for social interaction with other children.

In this case you can expect to see significant improvement in three to five days, even with children who bite many times a day (or try to). On the other hand, if the child continues to bite, it is likely you have been inconsistent in your actions, or perhaps you have missed an important reason or two. Your Action Plan then needs to be adjusted. Review the Seven Questions, review all Injury and Incident reports, and have another conversation with parents and caregivers to decide what additional changes to make.

If after one month the child is still biting, it is probable that an evaluation by a health care professional, a parent educator, or a family therapist may be necessary to get at the root cause. All of your work toward determining the cause yourself will be of great interest to this professional, so provide him or her with copies of your notes and the Action Plan. Do not hesitate to ask for professional help if the child is still struggling (or you are).

Action Plan Steps

1. Make observations with the Seven Questions in mind.
2. Document biting episodes.
3. Review Injury and Incident reports, observations, and notes with involved adults.
4. Write up an Action Plan.
5. Implement the Action Plan, with reviews every few days to make any needed adjustments.

Conclusion

Pat yourself on the back for making the effort to learn how to help the child who bites to get past this difficult time. Each developmental phase a child passes through has its own behaviors and needs that can be quite confounding. Parents and early childhood educators who have learned *how to observe, figure out solutions, and create an action plan* stand a fine chance of helping a child navigate the changes. Providing your own child or a child in your care with tools for expressing feelings and getting along with others is a gift that will last a lifetime. Congratulations on what you are about to accomplish!

Make as many copies of this worksheet as you need.

Action Plan Worksheet		
Child's Name/Age _____		Today's Date _____
7 Questions	**Describe the Situation**	**Design the Solutions**
1. Stage of Development		
2. Past Experiences and Recent Changes		
3. Verbal Skills		
4. Physical Condition		

(Continued on next page)

Action Plan Worksheet (continued)		
7 Questions	**Describe the Situation**	**Design the Solutions**
5. Temper- ament		
6. Physical Environment		
7. Limit Setting		

Solving Other Hurtful Behaviors with the Seven Questions

You can use Instructive Intervention and the Seven Questions to address all manner of hurtful behaviors, even with older children. You have learned to think like a consultant or detective to uncover all of the reasons behind children's distressing behavior. Whether it is grabbing, hitting, kicking, pushing, spitting, or scratching, children act on their feelings in harmful ways for a constellation of reasons. It is never as simple as one reason. A targeted type of problem solving to uncover the reasons gives parents and teachers a framework for thinking things through before taking actions that may do more harm than good. Some of the reasons for the child's behavior may be out of your control. However, there are usually many proactive things you can do to reduce stressors, as well as steps you can take to help the child learn a more appropriate way to deal with others in stressful situations and express difficult feelings without hurting someone else. Most of the time, the solution has more to do with changes made by adults rather than children. Once adults adjust their expectations, routines, environment, etc., children are better equipped to deal with other people, both adults and children, in more positive ways.

If your child or a child in your care hurts others in any way, work through the Seven Questions (below), refer to Instructive Intervention in the second chapter, and create an Action Plan that fits your situation. Don't skip any questions or you may miss the most potent underlying reason for the recurring behavior. Start with identifying whether or not the concerning behavior is age appropriate and move on to the other questions from there. You will find that there is always something more you can do to improve the situation and always something more you can say to be more effective during your intervention.

Summary of the Seven Questions

1. How much of the child's behavior is related to typical social/emotional development?
   - *Are my expectations in line with the child's current developmental capabilities?*
   - *What are some proactive things I can do to help the child develop empathy, impulse control, and a broader vocabulary of words for feelings?*

2. Are there some past or present experiences that have influenced this behavior?
   - *Am I minimizing the emotional impact of some recent changes in the child's life?*
   - *What changes do I need to make to reduce stressors that are within my control?*

3. Is the child's physical condition a contributing factor?

- *Is there an underlying health problem that is causing irritability?*

- *Is lack of sleep or hunger part of the problem?*

4. Is the lack of verbal skills causing frustration?
- *Does this child seem to be struggling to communicate clearly?*

- *Should I proactively use more speech and language tools with this child: extension, commentary, self-talk, starter phrases, wondering, etc.?*

5. What role does this child's temperament play in this behavior?
- *Are any of the temperament traits contributing to this behavior problem?*

- *Am I putting the child in situations that are overwhelming his or her ability to deal with people in a positive way due to a lack of "good fit"?*

6. How does the physical environment of home and/or school affect the child's behavior?
- *Are struggles made worse by lack of items, space, or softness, stressful challenges, etc.?*

- *Could typical struggles be caused by sensory over-stimulation?*

7. What kind of limit setting is the child experiencing?
- *Am I using clear, consistent, authoritative limit-setting philosophy?*

- *Is my style calm and firm, or do I find myself frequently resorting to shouting, sarcasm, threats, force, shame, etc.?*

How to intervene during other types of hurtful behaviors

After making any necessary changes based on the Seven Questions above, polish up your intervention techniques by remembering the steps below.

After intervening to stop the hurtful action, separate the children as necessary and help the victim. Then:

- Use active listening to reflect everyone's feelings
- Define the problem
- Clarify the limit
- Provide a relevant solution
- Teach verbal tools
- Put closure on the situation.

(Photocopy and distribute the Biting Solution Pocket Guide on page 121. Review the Puppet Show Script on page 22.)

Instructive Intervention for pushing: Toddler

"Allison, you wanted the bear and you felt frustrated when Milo wouldn't give it to you, so you pushed him down. He hurt his head on the floor, which made him sad, right Milo? I'm glad you're feeling better now, Milo. Allison, I can't let you near Milo when you push him. We always touch people gently. Allison, look at me. . . . If you feel like pushing because you want a toy that someone is using, you can take a big breath and ask 'Mine?'

Then Milo will know you are waiting for the next turn. I know it's hard to wait so you can sit with me. I'll help you wait. What do you want to play with until Milo is done with the bear? When he brings it over, it'll be your turn."

Instructive Intervention for hitting: Two-year-old
"Andres, it bothered you when Patrick got close to your puzzle and you hit him. That hurt Patrick and made him angry . . . and then Patrick hit you back! It was really hard for both of you, but hurting people is not okay; you must always touch people gently. Listen, . . . if you feel like hitting, just squeeze your hands into a tight fist like this [demonstrate], hold them down, and say, 'Move over' or 'Don't do that to me.' You can also use a loud voice to say 'Help!' and I'll come help you. Understand? Great! Now, let's go find two puzzles and some space at the table for each of you."

Instructive Intervention for kicking: Three-year-old
"So, Megan, the problem is that you felt disappointed because Riley said she didn't want to dance with you, and it hurt your feelings. Then you got mad and kicked Riley in the leg, so she got hurt and felt sad, too. Listen to me, Megan, you can stomp your foot when you feel upset, but kicking is never okay. If Riley says she won't dance with you, can you think of another idea, a better solution to your problem? [Possible ideas to discuss: Megan can ask Riley why she doesn't want to dance with her. Maybe Riley's worried Megan will accidentally bump into her because of her exuberance, so perhaps Megan can dance farther apart; she can find someone else to dance with; she can offer Riley another play idea; or she can talk to an adult about it.] Those are some good ideas. Which one will you try first next time? . . . I'm glad we talked this through and you both feel better now. What would you like to do next?"

Conclusion

Whenever you are faced with a persistent and frustrating behavioral issue, resist the urge to give in to your emotions and simply blame the child. Chances are the child is missing some valuable life lessons or dealing with some ill-fitting situations that are negatively impacting his or her ability to manage daily life in a positive way. Take a deep breath, determine what kinds of changes are within your control, and then use your best efforts to stay calm, age-appropriate, intentional, and consistent in your responses. Looking back on it, whether you are a parent or teacher, you will have the pleasure of knowing how to use your new consulting skills—to gather critical information by listening and observing and to put together a customized action plan with thoughtful changes and interactions that meet everyone's needs.

Appendix I

Temperament Worksheet Form, pages 58–60
Action Plan Worksheet Form, pages 111–112
Injury Report Form, page 118
Incident Report Form, page 118

Injury Report

Name of injured child:_____   Child's age:___yrs, ___months

Date of incident: ___/___/___   Day of week: _____   Time of day: _____

Location of incident: _____

Describe what happened before and during the incident: _____

_____

_____

_____

Describe the injury: _____

_____

Describe the treatment: _____

_____

Names of adults in the room at the time of the incident:_____

Notes: _____

_____

Reported by: _____ (caregiver/teacher)

Received by: _____ (parent) Date: _____

Incident Report: Attempted but interrupted biting

Child attempting to bite: _____   Age: ___ yrs, ___ months

Date of incident: ___/___/___   Day of week: _____   Time of day: _____

Target child (or adult): _____   Age:___ yrs, ___ months

Location of incident: _____

Activity/Circumstances: _____

_____

Comments/Assessment of situation: _____

_____

Describe the intervention: _____

_____

Reported by:_____ (caregiver/teacher)

Appendix II

Turn-taking Tips

In everyday situations, find opportunities to model the concept of turn-taking:

- "I'm through brushing my hair. Do you want a turn with the brush?"
- "I've been stirring this spaghetti sauce for a long time. Would you like a turn now?"
- "Let's play ball. Your turn….my turn….your turn….my turn…"
- "Let's put this puzzle together. I'll try this piece here…yes, it fits. Your turn…."
- "When I'm finished with the sponge, do you want a turn with it?"
- "You can have a turn with the truck in three more minutes. Let's set the egg timer."
- "I'll be done with your sister's hair in five minutes and then it will be your turn."

Help children figure out how to determine when a turn begins and when a turn ends:

- "Look, Sonia got off the trike; her turn is over. Do you want to ride the trike now?"
- "You want a turn with a red shovel? Let's try to find one that isn't being used."
- "You put the doll down; that was the end of your turn. Analena picked up the doll; now it is her turn. When she is all done playing with it and she puts it down, you can have another turn."
- While reading a picture book, point out situations where the characters take turns.

Point out the times that adults must patiently wait for a turn:

- "Let's pull a number ticket here at the meat counter. The butcher will call our number when he is ready to give us a turn. While we're waiting, let's look at the fish."
- "Look, so many cars in line at the bridge! Everyone wants a turn to cross the river."
- "You and I will wait right here on the curb. Let's watch the light; it will tell us when it's our turn to cross the street."
- "Here we are at the bank, waiting for our turn at the window. After the lady in front of us is done getting her money, it will be our turn to get our money."

Appendix III

Sample Starter Phrases
Gaining a child's attention

- [Child's name], listen . . .
- Here's a thought . . .
- How about this idea . . .
- I've got an idea for you . . .
- What do you think about this . . .
- I wonder if . . .
- Maybe this idea would work . . .
- Ah-ha, I see what the problem is . . .

Active Listening Feeling Phrases
Reflect the feeling, describe the situation

- "You feel very____ because . . ."
- "It sounds like you feel _____ because . . ."
- "You're having trouble with ____ and that feels ___."
- "It seems to me that you feel ____ because . . ."
- "Looks like you feel _____ because . . ."

Difficult Feelings Words
A variety of words to describe intense feelings

Angry	Mad	Impatient
Frustrated	Furious	Disappointed
Sad	Scared	Irritated
Worried	Upset	Bored
Embarrassed	Annoyed	Confused

Appendix IV

Biting Solution Pocket Guide	
Use Active Listening	To bitten child: "That hurt and now you're sad." To biter: "You were frustrated and angry."
Define the problem	"The problem is you both wanted to play with the _____."
Clarify the limit	"Listen, . . . we always touch people gently, even when we're angry. If you bite people, I won't let you near them."
Provide solution for expressing feelings	"Whenever you feel frustrated and angry, take a big, deep breath and blow it out."
Provide solution for expressing needs	"Next time you feel frustrated and angry, you can say, 'I need a turn' in a loud voice. Then find me/a teacher to help you."
Provide closure	"I'm glad you're all done biting. Let's go . . ."

Appendix V

Lyrics to Two Songs that Teach Alternatives to Biting

 *"We Don't Put Our Teeth on People"*
by The 2 Tones (© 2011)

When I get mad I know what to do
I yell with my voice and I stomp with my shoe.
But never, ever will I bite on you,
'cause we don't put our teeth on people.

We use our teeth to chomp and chew
on apples and carrots and cookies, too.
But never, ever will I bite on you,
'cause we don't put our teeth on people.

When I get angry, when I don't get my way,
I need to remember what I learned today, so I say . . .

No matter what, no matter who
Animals, friends, and teachers, too.
Never, ever will I bite on you,
'cause we don't put our teeth on people.

When I get angry, when I don't get my way
I need to remember what I learned today, so I say . . .

When I get mad I know what to do.
I yell with my voice and I stomp with my shoe.
But never, ever will I bite on you
'cause we don't put our teeth on people.

(The music for this song is available for purchase on *www.cdbaby.com*.)

"*Someone You Love (The Hug Song)*"
by The 2 Tones (© 2005)

Give someone you love a hug today.
Give someone you love a hug today.
Tell them that they're special in all they do and say.
Give someone a hug today.

Sing someone you love a song today.
Sing someone you love a song today.
Tell them that they're special in all they do and say.
Sing someone a song today.

Tell someone you love *I love you* today.
Tell someone you love *I love you* today.
Tell them that they're special in all they do and say.
Tell someone *I love you* today.

Give someone you love a hug today.
Give someone you love a hug today.
Tell them that they're special in all they do and say.
Give someone a hug today.
Sing someone a song today.
Tell someone *I love you* today.
Give someone a hug today.

(The music for this song is available for purchase on *www.cdbaby.com*.)

Appendix VI

References

American Sign Language. *www.signingsavvy.com*. Search the sign language dictionary by keying in a word or phrase that you wish to use with the child in your care. Learn new signs.

Ames, L., and Ilg, F. *Your Two-Year-Old: Terrible or Tender.* New York: Dell Publishing Co., 1980

Appelbaum, Maryln, Dr. *No More Biting!* Sugar Land, Texas: Appelbaum Publishing, 2006

Aron, Elaine N., Ph.D. *The Highly Sensitive Child.* New York: Broadway Books, 2002

Bergen, Doris, Reid, Rebecca, Torelli, Louis. *Educating and Caring for Very Young Children, The Infant/Toddler Curriculum.* New York: Teachers College Press, Columbia University, 2001

Brazelton, T. Berry, M.D. *Toddlers and Parents: A Declaration of Independence,* 2nd ed. New York: Dell Publishing Co., 1989

Brazelton, T. Berry, M.D., and Joshua D. Sparrow, M.D. *Sleep: The Brazelton Way.* New York: Da Capo Press, 2003

Brazelton, T. Berry, M.D., and Joshua D. Sparrow, M.D. *Touchpoints: Birth to Three,* 2nd ed. New York: Da Capo Press, 2006

Bredekamp, Sue. *Developmentally Appropriate Practice in Early Childhood Programs Serving Children From Birth Through Age 8.* Washington, D.C.: National Association for the Education of Young Children, 1987

Bruni, Maryanne. *Fine Motor Skills for Children with Down Syndrome,* 2nd ed. Bethesda, Maryland: Woodbine House, 2006

Crary, Elizabeth, M.S., *Dealing with Disappointment: Helping Kids Cope When Things Don't Go Their Way.* Seattle, Wash.: Parenting Press, 2003

Crary, Elizabeth, M.S. *STAR Parenting Tales and Tools: Respectful Guidance Strategies to Increase Parenting Effectiveness & Enjoyment.* Seattle, Wash.: Parenting Press, 2011

Crary, Elizabeth, M.S. *Without Spanking or Spoiling: A Practical Approach to Toddler and Preschool Guidance,* 2nd ed. Seattle, Wash.: Parenting Press, 1993

Cuthbertson, Joanne and Schevill, Susie. *Helping Your Child Sleep Through the Night.* New York: Doubleday, 1985

Galinsky, Ellen. *Mind in the Making: The Seven Essential Life Skills Every Child Needs.* New York: William Morrow Paperbacks, 2010

Gonzales-Mena, Janet and Eyer, Dianne Widmeyer. *Infants, Toddlers and Caregivers: A Curriculum of Respectful, Responsive, Relationship-Based Care and Education,* 9th ed. New York: McGraw-Hill, 2011

Greenman, Jim. *Caring Spaces, Learning Places: Children's Environments that Work.* Redmond, Wash.: Exchange Press, Inc., 2005

Huntley, Rebecca. *The Sleep Book for Tired Parents.* Seattle, Wash.: Parenting Press, 1991

Jones, Elizabeth, ed. *Growing Teachers: Partnerships in Staff Development*. Washington, D.C. : National Association for the Education of Young Children, 1993

Kaiser, Barbara and Rasminsky, Judy Sklar. *Challenging Behavior in Young Children*, 2nd ed. Boston: Allyn & Bacon, 2006

Karp, Harvey, M.D. *The Happiest Toddler on the Block*, rev. New York: Bantam, 2008

Kinnell, Gretchen. *No Biting, Policy and Practice for Toddlers Programs*, 2nd ed. St. Paul, Minn.: Redleaf Press, 2002

Kumin, Libby, Ph.D. *Early Communication Skills for Children with Down Syndrome: A Guide for Parents and Professionals*, 3rd ed. Bethesda, Maryland: Woodbine House, 2012

Lansky, Vicky. *Feed Me, I'm Yours*. Minnetonka, Minn.: Meadowbrook Press, 1981

Levine, Joni, M.Ed., *The Everything Parent's Guide to Tantrums*. Avon, Mass.: Adams Media, 2005

Lieberman, Alicia F., Ph.D. *The Emotional Life of the Toddler*. New York: The Free Press, 1993

MacKenzie, Robert J., Ed.D. *Setting Limits with Your Strong-Willed Child*. New York: Three Rivers Press, 2001

Mitchell, Grace, Ph.D., and Dewsnap, Lois. *Help! What Do I Do About . . . ?* New York: Scholastic, 1993

Nelsen, Jane, Ed.D., Erwin, Cheryl, M.A., Duffy, Roslyn Ann. *Positive Discipline: The First Three Years*, 2nd ed. New York: Three Rivers Press, 2007

Neville, Helen F. *Is This a Phase? Child Development & Parent Strategies, Birth to 6 Years*. Seattle, Wash.: Parenting Press, 2007

Neville, Helen F. *Temperament Tools: Working with Your Child's Inborn Traits*. Seattle, Wash.: Parenting Press, 1998

Satter, Ellyn, R.D, A.C.S.W. *Child of Mine: Feeding with Love and Good Sense*, 3rd edition. Boulder, Colo.: Bull Publishing Co., 2000

Shick, Lyndall, M.A. *Understanding Temperament: Strategies for Creating Family Harmony*. Seattle, Wash.: Parenting Press, 1998

Sohn, Alan, Ed.D., and Grayson, Cathy, M.A. *Parenting Your Asperger Child: Individualized Solutions for Teaching Your Child Practical Skills*. New York: A Perigee Book (Penguin), 2005

Turecki, Stanley, M.D., and Turner, Leslie. *The Difficult Child*, 2nd ed. New York: Bantam, 1989

Whitebook, Marcy and Sakai, Laura. *By a Thread: How Child Care Centers Hold On to Teachers, How Teachers Build Lasting Careers*. Kalamazoo, Michigan: W. E. Upjohn Institute for Employment Research, 2004

Winders, Patricia C. *Gross Motor Skills in Children with Down Syndrome*. Bethesda, Maryland: Woodbine House, 1997

Wyckoff, Jerry, Ph.D., and Unell, Barbara C. *Discipline Without Shouting or Spanking*, 2nd ed. Minnetonka, Minn.: Meadowbrook Press, 2002

Young Children. The journal of the National Association for the Education of Young Children (NAEYC), Washington, D.C., published five times per year

Index